History 4
Learning Coach Guide

Part 2

About K12 Inc.

K12 Inc. (NYSE: LRN) drives innovation and advances the quality of education by delivering state-of-the-art digital learning platforms and technology to students and school districts around the world. K12 is a company of educators offering its online and blended curriculum to charter schools, public school districts, private schools, and directly to families. More information can be found at K12.com.

978-1-60153-319-7

PPrinted by LSC Communications, Kendallville, IN, USA, May 2019.

Table of Contents

Learning Coach Guide
Lesson 1: Livingstone and Stanley in Africa

A man of curiosity and faith, Scottish doctor David Livingstone went to Africa as a missionary. He explored the interior of Africa and was missing for several years. Reporter Henry Stanley found him and later traveled with him. The journeys and reports of both men excited European interest in Africa.

Lesson Objectives

- Describe "imperialism" as the push to create empires overseas.
- Recognize that the "age of imperialism" came at the end of the nineteenth and early twentieth centuries.
- Explain that industrial nations wanted colonies for more resources and naval bases.
- Describe Africa as nearly completely colonized by different European nations.
- Explain the phrase "the sun never sets on the British empire".
- Identify some famous figures and events in this period (David Livingstone, Henry Stanley, Ferdinand de Lesseps, Rudyard Kipling, Kaiser Wilhelm, Theodore Roosevelt; building of Suez Canal; the Spanish-American War).
- Locate on a map some of the major colonies of Great Britain, France, Germany, and territories owned by the United States.
- Define *imperialism* as the drive to create empires overseas.
- Explain that David Livingstone was a Scottish missionary and doctor who explored Africa, and that Henry Stanley was sent to find him.
- Recognize the phrase "Dr. Livingstone, I presume?" as the first words spoken by Stanley to Livingstone in Africa.
- Explain that reports about the adventures of Livingstone and Stanley excited European interest in Africa.

PREPARE

Approximate lesson time is 60 minutes.

Materials

For the Student

- Colonial Africa Color Map
- Africa in the Age of Imperialism
- map of Colonial Africa, circa 1900
- map of Colonial Africa, circa 1900 (color)

Keywords and Pronunciation

imperialism : The drive to build an empire or gain colonies overseas.

missionary : A person who spreads his or her religious faith to others.

Zambezi (zam-BEE-zee)

TEACH

Activity 1: The Scramble for Africa (Online)

Instructions

Your student may complete this activity alone or with your help.

Activity 2: History Journal (Offline)

Instructions

With your student, read the History Journal entry for today's lesson and compare it with the sample paragraph below. Did it include the most important parts of the lesson?

David Livingstone was a famous explorer. He was a doctor. He was also a missionary. He explored Africa. People in Europe liked to hear about his adventures. They did not hear from him for a long time and thought he was dead. A reporter named Henry Stanley went to find him. When he finally found him, he said, "Dr. Livingstone, I presume?" People in Europe got very interested in Africa. It was a time of imperialism. More and more Europeans began going to Africa.

Activity 3: Africa in the Age of Imperialism (Offline)

Instructions

Have your student complete the Africa in the Age of Imperialism activity sheet.

Answers:

1. Victoria Falls
2. imperialism
3. Mediterranean Sea
4. Egypt
5. "Dr. Livingstone, I presume?"
6. Great Britain and France

ASSESS

Lesson Assessment: Livingstone and Stanley in Africa (Online)

Students will complete an online assessment based on the lesson objectives. The assessment will be scored by the computer. The attached answer key is the most current and may not coincide with previously printed guides.

2

Learning Coach Guide
Lesson 2: The French and the Suez Canal

Eager to facilitate trade between Europe and Asia, the French sought permission from the ruler of Egypt to build a canal linking the Red Sea with the Mediterranean. Ten years later, one of the most important interocean waterways in the world opened. Colonial powers now had a swift route from Asia to Europe.

Lesson Objectives

- Locate the Mediterranean Sea, Isthmus of Suez, Gulf of Suez, Red Sea, and Suez Canal on a map.
- Explain that the Suez Canal connected the Mediterranean Sea and Red Sea, making it possible to travel much more quickly between Europe and Asia.
- Explain that the French built the Suez Canal.
- Identify Ferdinand de Lesseps as the French engineer in charge of building the Suez Canal.

PREPARE

Approximate lesson time is 60 minutes.

Materials

For the Student

- Map of the Suez Canal, 1869
- globe
- History Journal
- Mapping the Suez Canal

For the Adult

- Mapping the Suez Canal Answer Key

Keywords and Pronunciation

canal : A man-made waterway.

cholera (KAH-luh-ruh)

Ferdinand de Lesseps (furd-ee-NAHN duh lay-SEPS)

isthmus (IS-muhs) : a narrow strip of land with water on both sides that connects two larger pieces of landPhonetic pronunciationIS-mus

Suez (SOO-ez)

TEACH
Activity 1: Digging a Ditch in the Desert *(Online)*

Instructions

This main teaching activity is online. Your student may complete this activity alone or with your help.

Activity 2: History Journal (Offline)

Instructions

With your student, read the History Journal entry for today's lesson and compare it with the sample paragraph below. Did it include the most important parts of the lesson?

The Suez Canal connects the Mediterranean Sea and the Red Sea. The French built the Suez Canal. They wanted a faster way for ships to get from Europe to Asia. Ferdinand de Lesseps was the man in charge of building the canal. He had to dig through miles of sand. He had to find water for his workers to drink. It was very hard to build the canal, but finally the job was done. The Suez Canal is one of the greatest canals in the world. Many ships travel through it every year.

Activity 3: Mapping the Suez Canal (Offline)

Instructions

Have the student complete the Mapping the Suez Canal activity sheet. You will use this activity sheet as the assessment for today's lesson. Print the Answer Key to evaluate his work.

ASSESS

Lesson Assessment: The French and the Suez Canal (Online)

Review your student's responses on the Mapping the Suez Canal activity sheet and input the results online. The attached answer key is the most current and may not coincide with previously printed guides.

Mapping the Suez Canal

Name _____   Date _____

Mapping the Suez Canal

The building of the Suez Canal was an engineering marvel. It also had a great impact on world trade.

1. On the map below, label the following:

    - Mediterranean Sea   • Red Sea
    - Isthmus of Suez   • Suez Canal
    - Gulf of Suez

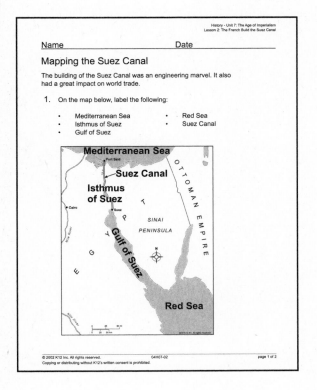

04H07-02   page 1 of 2

2. What two bodies of water does the Suez Canal connect?

    __Mediterranean Sea__   __Red Sea__

3. Which country built the Suez Canal? __France__

4. Who was the engineer in charge of building the Suez Canal?
    Ferdinand de Lesseps

5. What was an important outcome of the building of the Suez Canal? (Hint: Think "trade.")
    It made it possible to travel much more quickly between
    Europe and Asia.

6. Trace the shortest route a ship would have taken from England to China before the Suez Canal was built. In another color, trace the shortest route a ship could take from England to China after the canal was built.

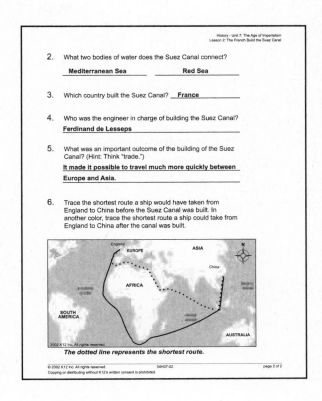

The dotted line represents the shortest route.

04H07-02   page 2 of 2

Mapping the Suez Canal

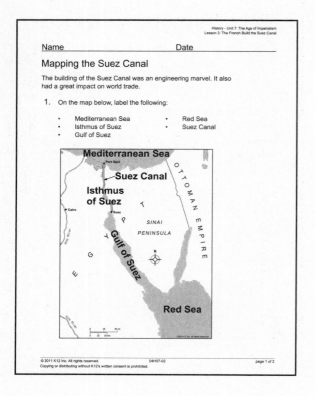

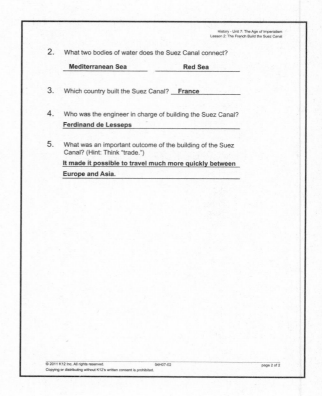

Learning Coach Guide
Lesson 3: Rudyard Kipling: Author and Advocate for Empire

Raised in India, Rudyard Kipling became both a publicist for the subcontinent and a cheerleader for the British Empire. He wrote verse, children's stories, and novels, celebrating a land he knew well and the nation that ruled it.

Lesson Objectives

- Locate India on the globe and describe it as a British colony in the 1800s.
- Recognize Rudyard Kipling as a great British writer who wrote about India.
- Explain that Kipling wrote children's stories.
- Explain that Kipling celebrated the British Empire in his writings.

PREPARE

Approximate lesson time is 60 minutes.

Materials

> For the Student
>
>> globe

TEACH
Activity 1: India, the Jewel in the British Crown *(Online)*
Instructions

This main teaching activity is online. Your student may complete this activity alone or with your help.

Activity 2: History Journal *(Offline)*
Instructions

Your student will answer five questions for today's History Journal entry. You will use the History Journal to assess his understanding of this lesson.

Answers:

1. India was a British colony.
2. Kipling was a British writer.
3. India was the subject of most of Kipling's work.
4. Kipling wrote for children (as well as for adults).
5. Kipling celebrated the British Empire in his writings.

Activity 3: News of Kipling (Offline)

Instructions

Have your student write a short newspaper article about Rudyard Kipling.

ASSESS

Lesson Assessment: Rudyard Kipling: Author and Advocate for Empire

(Online)

Review your student's responses in the History Journal entry and input the results online. The attached answer key is the most current and may not coincide with previously printed guides.

Name _____   Date _____

Lesson Assessment Answer Key

Rudyard Kipling: Author and Advocate for Empire

Answers:

1. India was a British colony.

2. Kipling was a British writer.

3. India was the subject of most of Kipling's work.

4. Kipling wrote for children (as well as for adults).

5. Kipling celebrated the British Empire in his writings.

Learning Coach Guide
Lesson 4: Germany's "Place in the Sun"

The late nineteenth and early twentieth centuries saw a Germany on the rise. Kaiser Wilhelm II was determined that the young German nation should obtain its "place in the sun." Germany established colonies in Africa and Asia, and a strong German navy to protect them.

Lesson Objectives

- Explain that Germany was becoming a powerful industrial nation.
- Identify Kaiser Wilhelm II as the emperor of Germany.
- Explain that Kaiser Wilhelm II wanted Germany to be a great nation with overseas colonies and a strong navy.
- Explain that Great Britain, France, and other European nations grew fearful of German ambition.

PREPARE

Approximate lesson time is 60 minutes.

Materials

> For the Student
>
>> globe
>>
>> 🖥 map of Colonial Africa, circa 1900

Lesson Notes

Kaiser Wilhelm II forced Bismarck to resign. Wilhelm II reigned from 1888 to 1918.

Keywords and Pronunciation

Bremerhaven (BREH-mur-hah-vuhn)

kaiser (KIY-zur) : Emperor of Germany.

Wilhelm (VIL-helm)

TEACH
Activity 1: The Kaiser Takes Charge *(Online)*

Instructions

This main teaching activity is online. Your student may complete this activity alone or with your help.

Activity 2: History Journal *(Offline)*

Instructions

With your student, read the History Journal entry for today's lesson and compare it with the sample paragraph below. Did it include the most important parts of the lesson?

Kaiser Wilhelm was the emperor of Germany. He wanted Germany to be a great nation. He bragged about Germany a lot. He wanted the Germans to have the best navy. He wanted a very strong army and lots of industry. He thought that German should have colonies. Countries like Great Britain and France were worried. They were worried that the Kaiser Wilhelm was going to war.

Activity 3: Carving up Africa (Offline)

Instructions

Your student will complete an activity that reinforces the colonization of Africa by European powers.

Answers:

1. Great Britain and France
2. Ethiopia and Liberia
3. Portuguese Guinea, Angola, and Portuguese East Africa
4. Spain, Italy
5. Belgian Congo
6. Great Britain's
7. Spain

ASSESS

Lesson Assessment: Germany's "Place in the Sun" (Online)

Students will complete an online assessment based on the lesson objectives. The assessment will be scored by the computer. The attached answer key is the most current and may not coincide with previously printed guides.

Learning Coach Guide
Lesson 5: "A Splendid Little War": The Spanish-American War

Europeans weren't the only ones who expanded their reach in the Age of Imperialism. The United States fought a war to help Cuba gain independence from Spain and ended up with a few overseas territories of its own.

Lesson Objectives

- Describe the Spanish-American War as a war in which the United States gained overseas territories.
- Identify territories gained by the United States during the Spanish-American War (the Philippines, Guam, Puerto Rico).
- Identify Theodore Roosevelt as an American leader who helped free Cuba and was a strong advocate for America's military strength.

PREPARE

Approximate lesson time is 60 minutes.

Materials

    For the Student

        globe

        Teddy Roosevelt: Young Rough Rider by Edd Winfield Parks

Keywords and Pronunciation

Guam (gwahm)
Philippines (FIH-luh-peenz)
Puerto Rico (PWEHR-toh REE-koh)
San Juan (san wahn)
Santiago (san-tee-AH-goh)

TEACH
Activity 1: America Rebuilds (Online)
Instructions

This main teaching activity is online. Your student may complete this activity alone or with your help.

Activity 2: History Journal (Offline)

Instructions

With your student, read the History Journal entry for today's lesson and compare it with the sample paragraph below. Did it include the most important parts of the lesson?

The United States gained some territories overseas in the Spanish American War. Americans wanted to help Cuba win freedom from Spain. They wanted a navy base in Cuba, too. Teddy Roosevelt fought with his Rough Riders in Cuba. They charged up San Juan Hill and defeated the Spanish. The United States won the war. The Philippines, Guam, and Puerto became territories of the United States.

Activity 3: The Questions Is, "Who Was T.R.?" *(Offline)*
Instructions
Have your student imagine he's one of the writers for a quiz show. Next week's show is about American presidents. He's been assigned Theodore Roosevelt. In his History Journal, he should write a list of answers to the question, "Who was Theodore Roosevelt?"

Possible answers:

1. A U.S. president who was a sickly boy, but grew up to be a good athlete.
2. A rugged outdoorsman who once led the New York City police department.
3. A man who built up the U.S. Navy.
4. A man who thought the United States should become a world power and have a strong military.
5. A man of action who raised a cavalry regiment to go and fight in Cuba.
6. The leader of Roosevelt's Rough Riders.
7. A man who led a charge up San Juan Hill in Cuba.
8. The person who first used the phrase "a splendid little war."

ASSESS

Lesson Assessment: "A Splendid Little War": The Spanish-American War
(*Online*)
Students will complete an online assessment based on the lesson objectives. The assessment will be scored by the computer. The attached answer key is the most current and may not coincide with previously printed guides.

TEACH

Activity 4. Optional: "A Splendid Little War": The Spanish-American War *(Offline)*
Instructions
Check your library or local bookstore for *Teddy Roosevelt: Young Rough Rider* by Edd Winfield Parks, illustrated by Gray Morrow (New York: Aladdin Paperbacks, 1989).

Learning Coach Guide
Lesson 6: Unit Review and Assessment

The student will review this unit and take the unit assessment.

Lesson Objectives

- Demonstrate mastery of important knowledge and skills taught in previous lessons.
- Demonstrate mastery of important knowledge and skills in this unit.
- Explain that David Livingstone was a Scottish missionary and doctor who explored Africa, and that Henry Stanley was sent to find him.
- Explain that reports about the adventures of Livingstone and Stanley excited European interest in Africa.
- Locate the Mediterranean Sea, Isthmus of Suez, Gulf of Suez, Red Sea, and Suez Canal on a map.
- Explain that the Suez Canal connected the Mediterranean Sea and Red Sea, making it possible to travel much more quickly between Europe and Asia.
- Explain that the French built the Suez Canal.
- Identify Ferdinand de Lesseps as the French engineer in charge of building the Suez Canal.
- Locate India on the globe and describe it as a British colony in the 1800s.
- Recognize Rudyard Kipling as a great British writer who wrote about India.
- Explain that Germany was becoming a powerful industrial nation.
- Identify Kaiser Wilhelm II as the emperor of Germany.
- Explain that Kaiser Wilhelm II wanted Germany to be a great nation with overseas colonies and a strong navy.
- Explain that Great Britain, France, and other European nations grew fearful of German ambition.
- Recognize that the "age of imperialism" came at the end of the nineteenth and early twentieth centuries.
- Explain that industrial nations wanted colonies for more resources and naval bases.
- Describe Africa as nearly completely colonized by different European nations.
- Explain the phrase "the sun never sets on the British empire".
- Locate on a map some of the major colonies of Great Britain, France, Germany, and territories owned by the United States.

PREPARE

Approximate lesson time is 60 minutes.

TEACH
Activity 1: The Age of Imperialism (Offline)
Instructions
The student will review this unit and take the unit assessment.

Answers
[1] Dr. David Livingstone

[2] Henry Stanley

[3] France

[4] the Suez Canal

[5] Asia

[6] Great Britain

[7] India

[8] Rudyard Kipling

[9] Because the British Empire was so large, it was always morning somewhere in the empire.

[10] Kaiser Wilhelm, or Wilhelm II

[11] the navy

[12] the Spanish American War

[13] The Rough Riders

[14] territories overseas

Activity 2: History Journal Review (Offline)
Instructions
The student will use the History Journal to review for the unit assessment. You can help by asking questions based on the work in the journal.

Activity 3: Online Interactive Review (Online)
Instructions
The student will continue reviewing the unit by completing an online, interactive review.

ASSESS

Unit Assessment: The Age of Imperialism (Offline)
Students will complete an offline Unit Assessment. Print the assessment and have students complete it on their own. Use the answer key to score the assessment, and then enter the results online. The attached answer key is the most current and may not coincide with previously printed guides.

The Age of Imperialism

Name _____   Date _____

The Age of Imperialism

Read each question and its answer choices. Fill in the bubble in front of the best answer.

1. What is *imperialism*?
   - ⓐ the drive to create a capitalist economy
   - ● the push to create empires overseas
   - ⓒ the hope of creating a united country
   - ⓓ the ability to make and sell goods

2. A desire for _____ prompted industrial nations to seek overseas colonies.
   - ⓐ spices and gold
   - ⓑ democratic revolutions
   - ● more resources and naval bases
   - ⓓ scientific understanding of nature

3. What continent was almost completely colonized by European nations in the late nineteenth century?
   - ⓐ North America
   - ⓑ South America
   - ● Africa
   - ⓓ Asia

---

4. "I was a British doctor and missionary who traveled to Africa to explore, help the sick, and spread the Christian faith. Who am I?"
   - ⓐ Ferdinand de Lesseps
   - ● David Livingstone
   - ⓒ Rudyard Kipling
   - ⓓ Henry Stanley

5. What happened shortly after reports of the African adventures of Livingstone and Stanley were printed in newspapers?
   - ⓐ The Americans built the Suez Canal.
   - ⓑ Germany decided against building a navy.
   - ⓒ France made India a French colony.
   - ● The British began to colonize parts of Africa.

6. Who built the Suez Canal?
   - ⓐ the British, led by David Stanley
   - ⓑ the Americans, led by Theodore Roosevelt
   - ● the French, led by Ferdinand de Lesseps
   - ⓓ the Egyptians, led by Pasha Said

7. What two bodies of water did the Suez Canal connect?
   - ⓐ the Red Sea and the Persian Gulf
   - ● the Mediterranean Sea and the Red Sea
   - ⓒ the Atlantic Ocean and the Pacific Ocean
   - ⓓ the Atlantic Ocean and the Mediterranean Sea

---

8. Why was the Suez Canal built?
   - ● to reduce travel time between Europe and Asia
   - ⓑ to allow trading caravans easy access to Egypt
   - ⓒ to improve international relations between France and Egypt
   - ⓓ to make it easier to travel from Africa to South America

9. Which country benefited most from the construction of the Suez Canal?
   - ⓐ United States
   - ⓑ France
   - ⓒ Germany
   - ● Great Britain

10. How would India in the 1800s be described?
    - ⓐ a free and independent nation
    - ⓑ a colony of Germany
    - ● a colony of Great Britain
    - ⓓ an uninhabited and unexplored land

11. Who was Rudyard Kipling?
    - ⓐ an American explorer who traveled in Africa
    - ⓑ a British writer who wrote about Africa
    - ● a British writer who wrote about India
    - ⓓ a German leader who colonized India

---

12. Why was it said that the "sun never sets on the British Empire"?
    - ⓐ All of Britain's colonies were in the east, where the sun rises.
    - ● The British Empire was so large that it was always daytime somewhere.
    - ⓒ Japan, the "land of the rising sun," was a British colony.
    - ⓓ Great Britain invented and used daylight savings time in its empire.

13. Why was the Suez Canal so important to Great Britain?
    - ⓐ It employed thousands of British subjects.
    - ● It shortened the travel time to India.
    - ⓒ It brought a lot of national pride to the nation.
    - ⓓ It caused Germany to stop its naval buildup.

14. In the late nineteenth century, Germany was becoming a _____ nation.
    - ⓐ weak and backward
    - ● powerful industrial
    - ⓒ wealthy and divided
    - ⓓ poorly educated

15. Who reigned as emperor in Germany in the late nineteenth century?
    - ⓐ Otto von Bismarck
    - ● Kaiser Wilhelm II
    - ⓒ Czar Nicholas II
    - ⓓ Theodore Roosevelt

The Age of Imperialism

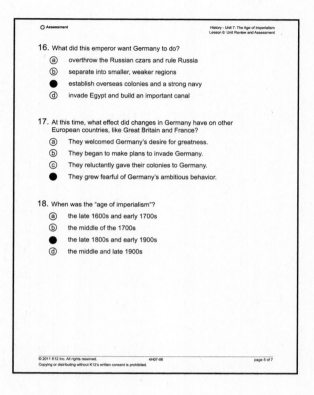

16. What did this emperor want Germany to do?
    - ⓐ overthrow the Russian czars and rule Russia
    - ⓑ separate into smaller, weaker regions
    - ● establish overseas colonies and a strong navy
    - ⓓ invade Egypt and build an important canal

17. At this time, what effect did changes in Germany have on other European countries, like Great Britain and France?
    - ⓐ They welcomed Germany's desire for greatness.
    - ⓑ They began to make plans to invade Germany.
    - ⓒ They reluctantly gave their colonies to Germany.
    - ● They grew fearful of Germany's ambitious behavior.

18. When was the "age of imperialism"?
    - ⓐ the late 1600s and early 1700s
    - ⓑ the middle of the 1700s
    - ● the late 1800s and early 1900s
    - ⓓ the middle and late 1900s

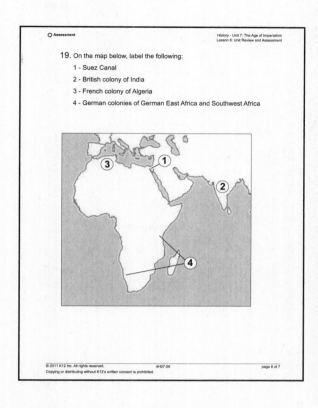

19. On the map below, label the following:
    1 - Suez Canal
    2 - British colony of India
    3 - French colony of Algeria
    4 - German colonies of German East Africa and Southwest Africa

20. Write a short paragraph about the Spanish-American War. In your paragraph:
    · Describe one outcome, or result, of the Spanish-American War.
    · Identify at least two overseas territories gained by the United States.
    · Name the American leader who helped free Cuba and tell how he felt about America's military.

    Begin your paragraph with a topic sentence. Write neatly in complete sentences. Check your spelling, capitalization, and punctuation. End your paragraph with a concluding sentence.

    _____
    _____
    _____
    _____
    _____
    _____
    _____
    _____
    _____
    _____
    _____
    _____
    _____
    _____
    _____

This essay question is worth forty points. Score the student's writing as follows:

- Ten points for describing one outcome, or result, of the Spanish-American War. Outcomes include:
    - The United States gained several overseas territories.
    - Cuba gained its independence from Spain.

- Ten points for identifying at least two overseas territories gained by the United States. Territories include:
    - The Philippines
    - Puerto Rico
    - Guam

- Ten points for naming Theodore Roosevelt as the American leader who helped free Cuba.

- Ten points for stating that Theodore Roosevelt felt strongly that the United States should have a strong military.

Learning Coach Guide
Lesson 1: Louis Pasteur

The great French chemist Louis Pasteur conducted wide-ranging research that had tremendous impact on the quality of modern life. Some of his most important work involved the effects of bacteria. Pasteur discovered the tiny organisms spoiled wine and milk. Later, he also discovered that bacteria sometimes spread human diseases.

Lesson Objectives

- Describe the late nineteenth and early twentieth centuries as an age of invention and enterprise.
- Explain that many great strides in medicine, industry, communication and transportation took place at this time.
- Identify some of the key innovators of the period (Pasteur, Samuel B. Morse, Thomas Edison, Alexander Graham Bell, Andrew Carnegie, Gustave Eiffel, Daimler and Benz, Henry Ford, Guglielmo Marconi, Orville and Wilbur Wright).
- Identify some of the major inventions, and innovations of the period (pasteurization, development of the telegraph, electric light, the telephone, steel industry, automobile, automobile factory, radio, airplanes, the Panama Canal).
- Describe Louis Pasteur as a great French scientist.
- Explain that Pasteur studied bacteria, and learned that it could sour food and spread disease.
- Explain that pasteurization is a process used on milk and other foods.
- Describe pasteurization as a process of using heat to kill bacteria.

PREPARE

Approximate lesson time is 60 minutes.

Materials

> For the Student
>> History Journal

Keywords and Pronunciation

Anton van Leeuwenhoek (AHN-tohn vahn LAY-ven-hook)

bacteria : a kind of microscopic organism.

germs : The common name for disease-causing bacteria.

Louis Pasteur (LOO-ee pas-TUR)

merci (MEHR-see)

Monsieur (muhs-yur)

pasteurization (pas-chuh-ruh-ZAY-shuhn) : A process of heating food to kill the germs that spoil it.

vintner : A wine maker.

TEACH
Activity 1: Pasteur Heats Things Up *(Online)*

Activity 2: History Journal *(Offline)*
Instructions
With your student, read the History Journal entry for today's lesson and compare it with the sample paragraph below. Did it include the most important parts of the lesson?

Louis Pasteur was a great French scientist. He studied bacteria. A wine maker came to see him. The vintner said that all his wine was being spoiled. Pasteur studied the wine through a microscope. He discovered that it was full of bacteria. He learned he could kill the bacteria by heating the wine. This heating process is called pasteurization. Today we pasteurize milk, cheese, and other foods to make them safe to eat.

Activity 3: In Honor of Pasteur *(Offline)*
Instructions
Have your student write a speech honoring Louis Pasteur. If time permits, he can practice and give the speech in front of an audience. You will evaluate your student's speech and use it as the assessment for this lesson.

Activity 4. Optional: Louis Pasteur *(Offline)*
Instructions
Let your student pick one quotation from Louis Pasteur to respond to.

ASSESS
Lesson Assessment: Louis Pasteur (*Online*)
Use the answer key to evaluate your students' essay and input the total point value in the assessment. The attached answer key is the most current and may not coincide with previously printed guides.

Lesson Assessment Answer Key

Louis Pasteur

Answers:

Answers will vary. Use the following grading rubric to award points for this question:

Did your student include in the speech the fact that Louis Pasteur was a great French scientist? *(10 points)*	
Did your student include in the speech the fact that Pasteur studied bacteria and learned that they could sour food and spread disease? *(10 points)*	
Did your student include in the speech the fact that pasteurization is a process of using heat to kill bacteria? *(10 points)*	
Did your student include in the speech the fact that pasteurization is used for milk and other foods, such as wine, cheese, eggs, and pickles? *(10 points)*	
Total *(40 points max)*:	

Learning Coach Guide
Lesson 2: Speeding It Up: Telegraphs, Sewing Machines, and Typewriters

The Age of Invention produced machines that could speed up all sorts or things up. The telegraph sped news across the country by wire. The typewriter made writing faster, and the sewing machine made it possible to make clothes a lot more quickly.

Lesson Objectives

- Explain that the telegraph was a means of rapid communication that used electric pulses to send messages by wire.
- Identify Samuel F. B. Morse as the inventor of the telegraph and the Morse code.
- Describe the Morse code as a series of clicks and pauses used to transmit messages.
- Describe the typewriter as the first practical writing machine.

PREPARE

Approximate lesson time is 60 minutes.

Materials

For the Student

Inventors: A Library of Congress Book by Martin Sandler

History Journal

Dot Dash Dot Activity Sheet

Keywords and Pronunciation

patent : The right to make, use, or sell an invention.

TEACH
Activity 1: Communication Speeds Up *(Offline)*

Instructions

This main teaching activity is offline. Your student will read part of the book *Inventors* by Martin W. Sandler, and answer questions based on the reading. Share the answers to the Get Ready, Reading Guide, and Show You Know questions with her.

Get Ready Answers:

1. Louis Pasteur discovered that bacteria caused wine to spoil.
2. Possible answers: "pasteurization" or heating the wine to a temperature that killed bacteria
3. Possible answers: milk, cheese, beer, pickles, soy sauce
4. vaccination

Reading Guide Answers for pages 7-13:

1. Possible answers: optimistic, hopeful, proud
2. the inventor
3. the railroad, the airplane, the automobile

Reading Guide Answers for pages 14-19:

1. A device that used electric pulses to transmit messages quickly by wire.
2. Samuel F. B. Morse
3. A system of clicks and pauses that allowed people to send messages
4. The telegraph was associated with speed. Newspapers wanted people to know that they could provide speedy news.
5. 400,000
6. the sewing machine
7. Isaac Singer
8. the typewriter
9. the problem of jamming
10. people who worked in offices

Show You Know Answers:

1. a communication device or system that used electric pulses to transmit messages quickly by wire
2. Samuel Morse
3. a system of clicks and pauses that allowed people to send messages
4. the typewriter

Activity 2: History Journal (Offline)

Instructions

With your student, read the History Journal entry for today's lesson and compare it with the sample paragraph below. Did it include the most important parts of the lesson?

Many great things have been invented in the United States. One of the most famous was the telegraph. Samuel Morse invented the telegraph. It used electricity to send messages over wires. People used Morse code to send the messages. Morse code used clicks to stand for letters. The typewriter was another great American invention. Machines such as the telegraph and typewriter changed lives everywhere.

Activity 3: Dot Dash Dot (Offline)

Instructions

Have your student work a little with Morse code using the Dot Dash Dot activity sheet.

ASSESS

Lesson Assessment: Speeding It Up: Telegraphs, Sewing Machines, and Typewriters (Offline)

Students will complete an offline assessment based on the lesson objectives. Print the assessment and have students complete it on their own. Use the answer key to score the assessment, and then enter the results online. The attached answer key is the most current and may not coincide with previously printed guides.

TEACH
Activity 4. Optional: Speeding It Up: Telegraphs, Sewing Machines, and Typewriters *(Online)*
Instructions
Your student can listen to actual Morse code at the National Association for Amateur Radio website.

Learning Coach Guide
Lesson 3: The Wizard of Menlo Park: Thomas Edison

One of the greatest inventors of all time, Thomas Edison invented the first practical electric lightbulb, the phonograph, the mimeograph, and thousands of devices. His "Invention Factory" became the model for modern industrial research laboratories.

Lesson Objectives

- Describe Edison as one of the greatest inventors of all time.
- Name the electric lightbulb as one of his inventions.
- Explain that Edison's "Invention Factory" became a model for industrial research laboratories.

PREPARE

Approximate lesson time is 60 minutes.

Materials

> For the Student
> > History Journal

Keywords and Pronunciation

phonograph : A device for playing music.

TEACH
Activity 1: Meet Thomas Edison *(Online)*
Instructions

This main teaching activity is online. Your student may want to complete this activity by herself, or you may want to join her at the computer as she reads about the Wizard of Menlo Park.

Activity 2: History Journal *(Offline)*
Instructions

With your student, read the History Journal entry for today's lesson and compare it with the sample paragraph below. Did it include the most important parts of the lesson?

Thomas Edison was the greatest American inventor. He was one of the greatest inventors of all time. He never gave up when he was trying to invent something. Edison's most famous invention is the electric lightbulb. But he invented many other things. Lots of scientists worked together to discover things in his Invention Factory. It was a big research lab. Today many companies have research labs based on Edison's Invention Factory.

Activity 3: The Invention Factory *(Offline)*

Instructions

Your student will write the presentation that a museum tour guide at the Invention Factory would give a tour group at the West Orange, New Jersey laboratories. You will use your student's presentation as the assessment for today's lesson.

ASSESS

Lesson Assessment: The Wizard of Menlo Park: Thomas Edison (*Online*)

Use the answer key to evaluate your students' Invention Factory essay and input the total point value in the assessment. The attached answer key is the most current and may not coincide with previously printed guides.

TEACH

Activity 4. Optional: The Wizard of Menlo Park: Thomas Edison *(Online)*

Instructions

Let your student explore the Edison National Historic Site: The Invention Factory (http://www.nps.gov/edis/inventionprocess/ENHS.html) online. This interactive website is packed with information about Edison's Invention Factory.

Name _____ Date _____

Lesson Assessment Answer Key

The Wizard of Menlo Park: Thomas Edison

Answers:

Answers will vary. Use the following grading rubric to award points for this question:

Did your student include in her presentation the fact that Edison was one of the greatest inventors of all time? *(10 points)*	
Did your student include in her presentation the fact that Edison invented the electric light bulb? *(10 points)*	
Did your student include in her presentation the fact that Edison's Invention Factory became a model for industrial research laboratories? *(10 points)*	
Total *(30 points total)*:	

Learning Coach Guide
Lesson 4: Alexander Graham Bell and the Telephone

In America, a spirit of invention filled the air in the late 1800s. One of the greatest inventions was the telephone. Alexander Graham Bell was the genius who brought this invention--and many others--to life.

Lesson Objectives

- Explain that the late 1800s was a time of many great inventions in America.
- Describe the telephone as a means of carrying speech over wires, and a major improvement in communication.
- Identify Alexander Graham Bell as the inventor of the telephone.

PREPARE

Approximate lesson time is 60 minutes.

Materials

For the Student

Inventors: A Library of Congress Book by Martin Sandler

pencils, colored, 16 colors or more

poster board

Keywords and Pronunciation

patent : The right to make, use, or sell an invention.

TEACH
Activity 1: Inventor of the Telephone (Offline)

Instructions

This main teaching activity is offline. Your student will read part of the book *Inventors* by Martin W. Sandler, and answer questions based on the reading. Share the answers to the Get Ready, Reading Guide, and Show You Know questions with her.

Get Ready Answers:

1. the telegraph
2. possible answers: an improved telegraph, an electric vote counter, a practical lightbulb, the phonograph
3. the industrial research lab modeled on Edison's Invention Factory

Reading Guide Answers for pages 24-27:

1. Accept any reasonable answer from the text, such as: a self-propelled hobby horse, a treadmill on which farm animals generate electricity, devices to make swimming easier, and crude flying machines.
2. the elevator
3. the air brake
4. Alexander Graham Bell

Reading Guide Answers for pages 28-33:

1. Possible answers: It could send speech, instead of clicks, over wires. Speech could be transmitted directly to home or office. No one had to decode a message or go to a station to pick the message up.
2. The telephone industry became large, employing more than 3 million people between 1876 and 1976.
3. Many poles and wires sprang up.
4. Possible answers: iron lung, hydrofoil, phonograph records, land-mine detectors, underwater sounding devices, innovations that help the development of the airplane.
5. Possible answers: George Washington Carver helped revive southern agriculture by proving that planting peanuts could improve the soil and introducing important products that could be made from the peanut crop. He also introduced many African American students to the world of science and technology.

Show You Know Answers:

1. It was a time of many inventions.
2. Alexander Graham Bell
3. a machine that sent speech over wires
4. Accept any reasonable answer, such as: a man of many interests and inventions

Activity 2: History Journal (Offline)

Instructions

With your student, read the History Journal entry for today's lesson and compare it with the sample paragraph below. Did it include the most important parts of the lesson?

Americans invented many new machines in the late 1800s. Some of them sound crazy. For example, someone invented a trolley car that looked like a horse. However, many inventions changed the world. One of the most famous inventors was Alexander Graham Bell. He invented the telephone. The telephone could carry voices over wires, so it was much better than the telegraph. Before long, cities all over the country had telephone wires running along the streets.

Activity 3: The Great Age of American Invention (Offline)

Instructions

Have your student create a poster that illustrates some of the inventions featured in the book *Inventors*.

ASSESS

Lesson Assessment: Alexander Graham Bell and the Telephone (*Offline*)

Students will complete an offline assessment based on the lesson objectives. Print the assessment and have students complete it on their own. Use the answer key to score the assessment, and then enter the results online. The attached answer key is the most current and may not coincide with previously printed guides.

Name _____   Date _____

Lesson Assessment Answer Key

Alexander Graham Bell and the Telephone

Answers:

10 points each.

The late 1800s was a time of many great **inventions** in America. In 1875, **Alexander Graham Bell** invented the telephone. The telephone was a major **improvement** in **communication**. It could carry **speech** a long distance over **wires**.

Learning Coach Guide
Lesson 5: Carnegie and Steel

The life of the inventive Scottish immigrant Andrew Carnegie is a rags-to-riches success story. After his impoverished father brought the family to America, 12-year-old Carnegie worked as a telegraph operator. He turned steel into a great industry and retired as the richest man in the world.

Lesson Objectives

- Describe Andrew Carnegie as an industrious Scottish immigrant.
- Explain that Carnegie built the steel industry in America and became one of the wealthiest men of his time.
- Describe steel as an extremely strong metal used to build railroads, buildings, and bridges.

PREPARE

Approximate lesson time is 60 minutes.

Materials

For the Student

📖 The Wonder of Steel

Inventors: A Library of Congress Book by Martin Sandler

TEACH
Activity 1: The Generous Man of Steel (Online)
Instructions
This main teaching activity is online. Your student may complete this activity alone or with your help.

Activity 2: History Journal (Offline)
Instructions
With your student, read the History Journal entry for today's lesson and compare it with the sample paragraph below. Did it include the most important parts of the lesson?

Andrew Carnegie was the man who built the steel industry in America. He came to America from Scotland when he was just a boy. His family did not have much money. Carnegie worked very hard. He worked as a telegraph operator. He also worked for a railroad. Then he made a huge fortune making steel. His steel was used in things like railroads and bridges. Andrew Carnegie became the richest man in the world. He gave away a lot of money to help other people.

Activity 3: The Wonder of Steel (Offline)

Instructions

Have your student read "The Wonder of Steel," pages 34-39, in the book *Inventors,* and complete the Wonder of Steel activity sheet.

Answers:

1. The new machines helped turn the United States into an agricultural giant.
2. Answers may vary, but should suggest that steel enabled cities to grow faster and larger.
3. roller coasters; Ferris wheels

ASSESS

Lesson Assessment: Carnegie and Steel (*Online*)

Students will complete an online assessment based on the lesson objectives. The assessment will be scored by the computer. The attached answer key is the most current and may not coincide with previously printed guides.

Learning Coach Guide
Lesson 6. Optional: Mr. Eiffel Builds a Tower

When it was built, in 1889, the Eiffel Tower was the tallest building in the world. Gustave Eiffel, a French engineer, designed the iron structure for the hundredth anniversary of the French Revolution. It has become a symbol of France.

Lesson Objectives

- Identify the Eiffel Tower from a set of images, and locate it in Paris, France.
- Describe Gustave Eiffel as the designer of the Eiffel Tower.
- Describe the Eiffel Tower as a symbol of France.
- Name two characteristics of the Eiffel Tower, such as it is made of iron; it is very tall; it has elevators.

PREPARE

Approximate lesson time is 60 minutes.

Materials

For the Student

History Journal

index cards, 4" x 6"

pencils, colored, 16 colors or more

Keywords and Pronunciation

Alexandre-Gustave Eiffel (GOUS-tahv IY-fuhl)

TEACH
Activity 1. Optional: Optional Lesson Instructions (Online)

Activity 2. Optional: A Monument For Paris (Online)
Instructions

This main teaching activity is online. Your student may want to complete this activity by herself, or you may want to join her at the computer as she reads about Gustave Eiffel's amazing monument.

Activity 3. Optional: History Journal (Offline)
Instructions

With your student, read the History Journal entry for today's lesson and compare it with the sample paragraph below. Did it include the most important parts of the lesson?

The Eiffel Tower is in Paris. It is a symbol of France and one of the most famous structures in the world. Gustave Eiffel designed the Eiffel Tower. He built it in 1889 to help celebrate the anniversary of the French revolution. Some people said the tower would fall down. But Eiffel built the tower anyway. At that time, it was the tallest tower in the world. Thousands of people went to see it when it opened. People still love to visit the Eiffel Tower today.

Activity 4. Optional: Greetings From the Eiffel Tower *(Offline)*

Instructions

Have your student make a postcard with an image and information about the Eiffel Tower.

Activity 5. Optional: Mr. Eiffel Builds a Tower *(Online)*

Instructions

Visit the Eiffel Tower online at the official site of the Eiffel Tower.

You may find the following particularly interesting:

Under "Visiting the Eiffel Tower"
Exploring the Eiffel Tower

Under "Children's Eiffel Tower"
Play with the Eiffel Tower

Learning Coach Guide
Lesson 7: Henry Ford Makes Cars Affordable

Two Germans and an American made automobiles the most important means of personal transportation all over the world. Gottlieb Daimler and Karl Benz perfected gasoline engines, and Henry Ford showed the world how to produce lots of affordable cars.

Lesson Objectives

- Associate Gottlieb Daimler and Karl Benz with the development of the gasoline engine.
- Identify Henry Ford as an American businessman who started assembly-line production of automobiles.
- Identify the Model T as a kind of car.
- Explain that Ford's assembly line factory made production faster and cheaper.

PREPARE

Approximate lesson time is 60 minutes.

Materials

  For the Student

    History Journal

    Model T: How Henry Ford Built a Legend by David Weitzman

Keywords and Pronunciation

Gottlieb Daimler (GAHT-leeb DIYM-lur)

Karl Benz (bents)

TEACH
Activity 1: Henry Ford and the Model T (Online)

Instructions

This main teaching activity is online. Your student may want to complete this activity by herself, or you may want to join her at the computer as she reads about Henry Ford and his Model T factory.

Activity 2: History Journal (Offline)

Instructions

With your student, read the History Journal entry for today's lesson and compare it with the sample paragraph below. Did it include the most important parts of the lesson?

Henry Ford invented a way to make cars faster and cheaper than ever before. His factory made an affordable car called the Model T. Workers on the Model T assembly line did the same job over and over again. Working on the assembly line was boring, but Henry Ford paid his workers well. That way, the workers could afford to buy cars.

Activity 3: Ford is Hiring! *(Offline)*

Instructions

Have your student demonstrate his knowledge of Ford and his production of cars by writing a "help wanted" ad.

ASSESS

Lesson Assessment: Henry Ford Makes Cars Affordable *(Online)*

Students will complete an online assessment based on the lesson objectives. The assessment will be scored by the computer. The attached answer key is the most current and may not coincide with previously printed guides.

TEACH

Activity 4. Optional: Henry Ford Makes Cars Affordable *(Offline)*

Instructions

David Weitzman's well-researched book, *Model T: How Henry Ford Built a Legend*, is filled with detailed black-and-white drawings, which will give your student a good look at Henry Ford in action.

Learning Coach Guide
Lesson 8: Marconi and the Radio

By the late 1800s the telegraph and the telephone provided quick long-distance communication, but both required wires connecting place to place. Was wireless communication possible? Italian inventor Guglielmo Marconi sent the first wireless telegraph signals both by land and across the sea. His "wireless" became the basis for the radio.

Lesson Objectives

- Describe the radio as a wireless form of communication.
- Identify Marconi as the first to send wireless signals through the air and across the Atlantic Ocean.
- Explain that the first radios were used by sinking ships to call for help.

PREPARE

Approximate lesson time is 60 minutes.

Materials

> For the Student
>> History Journal

Keywords and Pronunciation

Enrico Caruso (ayn-REE-koh kah-ROO-soh)
Guglielmo Marconi (gool-YEL-moh mahr-KOH-nee)

TEACH
Activity 1: Marconi: The Father of Radio (Online)
Instructions

This main teaching activity is online. Your student may want to complete this activity by herself, or you may want to join her at the computer as she reads how Marconi developed the "wireless telegraph."

Activity 2: History Journal (Offline)
Instructions

With your student, read the History Journal entry for today's lesson and compare it with the sample paragraph below. Did it include the most important parts of the lesson?

Guglielmo Marconi was the first person to send wireless signals all the way across the Atlantic Ocean. The telephone and telegraph were great inventions, but they needed wires. Marconi wanted a way to send messages through the air. People thought he was crazy, but he kept working on his invention. Finally he was able do send a signal across the ocean. At first, ships used his invention to send calls for help when they were sinking. Because of Marconi's great invention, we have radios today.

Activity 3: Marconi's Acceptance Speech *(Offline)*
Instructions
Have your student write Marconi's acceptance speech of the 1909 Nobel Prize in Physics.

ASSESS
Lesson Assessment: Marconi and the Radio (*Online*)
Students will complete an online assessment based on the lesson objectives. The assessment will be scored by the computer. The attached answer key is the most current and may not coincide with previously printed guides.

TEACH
Activity 4. Optional: Marconi and the Radio *(Online)*
Instructions
Visit the interactive activity at PBS's a Science Odyssey website to explore how Marconi's invention made it possible to send sound great distances through the air.

Learning Coach Guide
Lesson 9: First in Flight: Orville and Wilbur Wright

The train and automobile could move people by land at a mile a minute. But could man fly? By the late 1800s numerous industrious inventors were trying to figure that out. The Wright Brothers succeeded in Kitty Hawk, North Carolina.

Lesson Objectives

- Describe Orville and Wilbur Wright as the inventors of the first successful airplane.
- State that the first successful flight occurred at Kitty Hawk, North Carolina.
- Explain that after the Wrights' invention, more and more pilots took to the skies.

PREPARE

Approximate lesson time is 60 minutes.

Materials

For the Student

History Journal

🖳 The Wright Brothers in Time activity sheet

Pioneers of the Air by Molly Burkett

Keywords and Pronunciation

Aviation : The science of flying; air travel.

TEACH
Activity 1: Meet the Wright Brothers (Offline)

Instructions

This main teaching activity is offline. Your student will read part of the book *Inventors* by Martin W. Sandler, and answer questions based on the reading. Share the answers to the Get Ready, Reading Guide, and Show You Know questions with him.

Get Ready Answers:

1. the telephone
2. the electric lightbulb
3. Gottlieb Daimler and Carl Benz
4. Henry Ford
5. Guglielmo Marconi
6. to rescue ships at sea

Reading Guide Answers for pages 74-76:

1. balloons, wind tunnels, gliders
2. The Wright brothers launched their first successful flight.
3. Kitty Hawk, North Carolina
4. They were bicycle makers.
5. The first flight lasted 12 seconds and the plane traveled 120 feet.

Reading Guide Answers for pages 77-80:

1. They made three more successful flights on the same day.
2. 59 seconds, or less than a minute
3. 125 miles at 40 miles per hour
4. Possible answers: brave pilots, daredevil flyers, stunt flyers who took people for rides at county fairs.
5. Possible answers: Airplanes became weapons in war. Nations competed for control of the skies.

Show You Know Answers:

1. They invented the first successful airplane.
2. Kitty Hawk, North Carolina
3. No. Flying became more and more popular. Many pilots took to the skies.

Activity 2: History Journal (Offline)

Instructions

Read your student's History Journal entry for today's lesson. Check his answers with the ones below. You will use your student's work to assess his understanding of this lesson.

1. Who were the inventors of the first successful airplane?
2. Where did their first successful flight occur?
3. What happened in aviation after the Wrights' invention?

Answers:

1. Orville and Wilbur Wright were the inventors of the first successful airplane.
2. The Wright brothers' first successful flight occurred at Kitty Hawk, North Carolina.
3. After the Wright brothers' invention, more and more pilots took to the skies.

Activity 3: The Wright Brothers in Time (Offline)

Instructions

Your student will complete the Wright Brothers in Time activity sheet.

Activity 4: First in Flight: Orville and Wilbur Wright (Offline)

Instructions

Check your library or local bookstore for *Pioneers of the Air*, by Molly Burkett (Barrons Juveniles, 1998). Your student can read about the Wright brothers and other aviation pioneers in this magazine-style format book with full-color illustrations and concise text.

ASSESS

Lesson Assessment: First in Flight: Orville and Wilbur Wright (Online)

Review your student's responses in the History Journal entry and input the results online. The attached answer key is the most current and may not coincide with previously printed guides.

Lesson Assessment Answer Key

First in Flight: Orville and Wilbur Wright

Answers:

1. Orville and Wilbur Wright were the inventors of the first successful airplane.
2. The Wright brothers' first successful flight occurred at Kitty Hawk, North Carolina.
3. After the Wright brothers' invention, more and more pilots took to the skies.

Learning Coach Guide
Lesson 10: The Panama Canal

One of the greatest engineering feats in history, the Panama Canal connected the Atlantic and Pacific Oceans. Engineers struggled with porous ground, intense heat, flash floods, malaria, yellow fever and a host of other obstacles to create this pathway between the seas.

Lesson Objectives

- Locate the Isthmus of Panama on a map.
- Describe the Panama Canal as a waterway connecting the Atlantic and Pacific Oceans.
- Explain that Americans wanted to build the canal to shorten a ship's travel time between the east and west coasts of the United States.
- Name two obstacles the canal builders had to overcome, such as yellow fever, heat, construction of locks, and landslides.

PREPARE

Approximate lesson time is 60 minutes.

Materials

For the Student

🖥 Map of Panama

map, world

History Journal

Keywords and Pronunciation

Culebra (koo-LAY-brah)

isthmus (IS-muhs) : A narrow strip of land connecting two larger land areas.

locks : Compartments of water in a canal; the water level in a lock can be raised or lowered to allow a ship to pass through the canal.

William Gorgas (GOR-gas)

TEACH
Activity 1: Connecting Two Oceans (Online)

Instructions

This main teaching activity is online. Your student may want to complete this activity by herself, or you may want to join her at the computer as she reads about the Panama Canal.

Activity 2: History Journal (Offline)
Instructions
With your student, read the History Journal entry for today's lesson and compare it with the sample paragraph below. Did it include the most important parts of the lesson?

The Panama Canal is one of the greatest building projects in history. It joins the Atlantic and Pacific Oceans. The United States needed the canal so ships could get from the East Coast to the West Coast faster. So the United States sent many people to build the Panama Canal. They had to build huge locks to raise and lower ships. They had to blast through rocks. They drained swamps to get rid of mosquitoes and yellow fever. It was very hard, but finally the canal was finished.

ASSESS

Lesson Assessment: The Panama Canal (Offline)
Students will complete an online assessment based on the lesson objectives. The assessment will be scored by the computer. The attached answer key is the most current and may not coincide with previously printed guides.

TEACH
Activity 3: The Panama Canal (Online)
Instructions
Explore with your student a wealth of photographs and documents concerning the Panama Canal.

Learning Coach Guide
Lesson 11: Unit Review and Assessment

The student will review this unit and take the unit assessment.

Lesson Objectives

- Demonstrate mastery of important knowledge and skills in this unit.
- Explain that Pasteur studied bacteria, and learned that it could sour food and spread disease.
- Describe pasteurization as a process of using heat to kill bacteria.
- Describe the Morse code as a series of clicks and pauses used to transmit messages.
- Describe Edison as one of the greatest inventors of all time.
- Name the electric lightbulb as one of his inventions.
- Explain that Edison's "Invention Factory" became a model for industrial research laboratories.
- Describe Andrew Carnegie as an industrious Scottish immigrant.
- Explain that Carnegie built the steel industry in America and became one of the wealthiest men of his time.
- Associate Gottlieb Daimler and Karl Benz with the development of the gasoline engine.
- Explain that Ford's assembly line factory made production faster and cheaper.
- Describe the radio as a wireless form of communication.
- Identify Marconi as the first to send wireless signals through the air and across the Atlantic Ocean.
- Describe Orville and Wilbur Wright as the inventors of the first successful airplane.
- State that the first successful flight occurred at Kitty Hawk, North Carolina.
- Describe the Panama Canal as a waterway connecting the Atlantic and Pacific Oceans.
- Name two obstacles the canal builders had to overcome, such as yellow fever, heat, construction of locks, and landslides.
- Identify Alexander Graham Bell as the inventor of the telephone.
- Identify some of the key innovators of the period (Pasteur, Samuel B. Morse, Thomas Edison, Alexander Graham Bell, Andrew Carnegie, Gustave Eiffel, Daimler and Benz, Henry Ford, Guglielmo Marconi, Orville and Wilbur Wright).
- Identify some of the major inventions, and innovations of the period (pasteurization, development of the telegraph, electric light, the telephone, steel industry, automobile, automobile factory, radio, airplanes, the Panama Canal).

PREPARE

Approximate lesson time is 60 minutes.

TEACH
Activity 1: Can Do! An Age of Breakthroughs and Enterprise (Offline)
Instructions
The student will review this unit and take the unit assessment.

Activity 2: History Journal Review (Offline)
Instructions
The student will use the History Journal to review for the unit assessment. You can help by asking questions based on the work in the journal.

Activity 3: Online Interactive Review (Online)
Instructions
The student will continue reviewing the unit by completing an online, interactive review.

ASSESS

Unit Assessment: Can Do! An Age of Breakthroughs and Enterprise (Offline)
Students will complete an offline Unit Assessment. Print the assessment and have students complete it on their own. Use the answer key to score the assessment, and then enter the results online. The attached answer key is the most current and may not coincide with previously printed guides.

Can Do! An Age of Breakthroughs and Enterprise

Name _____ Date _____

Can Do! An Age of Breakthroughs and Enterprise

Read each question and its answer choices. Fill in the bubble in front of the word or words that best answer each question.

1. The telegraph transmitted message through:
   - (a) water, using a system of canals
   - ● wires, using a system of clicks and pauses
   - (c) air, using a highly developed radio
   - (d) telephone lines, using cable technology

2. Which important French scientist discovered that harmful bacteria spoil certain foods?
   - (a) Gustave Eiffel
   - ● Louis Pasteur
   - (c) Ferdinand de Lesseps
   - (d) Baron de Coubertin

3. That French scientist figured out a way to:
   - (a) keep wine from souring by using steel casks
   - ● kill bacteria by heating it
   - (c) avoid problems by rotating vineyards
   - (d) store wine at cool temperatures

4. Both Thomas Edison and Andrew Carnegie worked as telegraph operators. That meant they had to learn:
   - (a) pasteurization
   - (b) to use arc lights
   - (c) radio frequencies
   - ● Morse Code

5. Carnegie worked in the railroad industry, but how did Andrew Carnegie make his fortune?
   - (a) sewing machines
   - ● steel plants
   - (c) telephones
   - (d) typewriters

6. The "Wizard of Menlo Park" was one of the greatest inventors of all time. His most famous invention was the electric lightbulb. Who was the "Wizard of Menlo Park"?
   - (a) Alexander Graham Bell
   - ● Thomas Edison
   - (c) Samuel Morse
   - (d) Andrew Carnegie

7. What was one reason Thomas Edison was so productive?
   - (a) He had an automated assembly line that sped up production of his inventions.
   - (b) He used hundreds of typewriters and electric telegraphs inside his laboratories.
   - (c) He had a system of note-taking that was impossible for other businessmen to read.
   - ● He had an "invention factory" that became a model for research laboratories.

8. Which famous Scottish immigrant to America invented the telephone?
   - (a) Andrew Carnegie
   - ● Alexander Graham Bell
   - (c) Henry Ford
   - (d) Guglielmo Marconi

9. Which of the following "headlines" describes the accomplishment of the Wright brothers?
   - ● First in Flight
   - (b) More Model Ts
   - (c) Engineers of the Eiffel
   - (d) Pioneers in Sound

10. This industrious Scottish immigrant ended up giving away the fortune he made in the steel industry. Who was he?
    - (a) Alexander Graham Bell
    - (b) James Hargreaves
    - ● Andrew Carnegie
    - (d) Louis Pasteur

11. Where was the first successful airplane flight?
    - (a) Detroit, Michigan
    - (b) Paris, France
    - ● Kitty Hawk, North Carolina
    - (d) Menlo Park, New Jersey

12. A great engineering triumph connected the Atlantic and Pacific Oceans. What was that waterway called?
    - (a) the Suez Canal
    - ● the Panama Canal
    - (c) the Erie Canal
    - (d) the Grand Canal

13. Guglielmo Marconi tried to get someone to fund his invention in Italy, but no one was interested. He ended up going to England for help. What did he invent?
    - (a) electric vote counter
    - ● radio
    - (c) telephone
    - (d) telegraph

14. Which of Karl Benz and Gottlieb Daimler's inventions encouraged automobile production?
    - ● gas engine
    - (b) assembly line
    - (c) rapid steel production
    - (d) Model T

Can Do! An Age of Breakthroughs and Enterprise

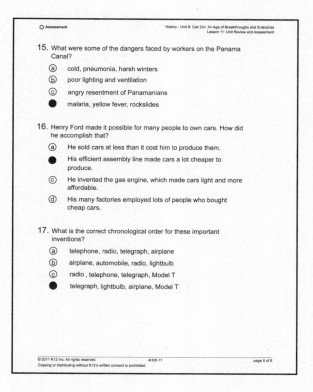

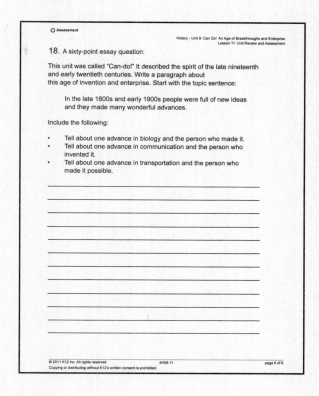

Scoring the Essay Question

This essay question is worth sixty points. Score the student's writing as follows:

- Award twenty points for explaining that Pasteur discovered harmful bacteria spoiled food and invented the process of heating the bacteria to kill it, pasteurization.

- Award twenty points for naming the telegraph invented by Samuel B. Morse, or the radio invented by Guglielmo Marconi, or the telephone invented by Alexander G. Bell as an advance in communication.

- Award twenty points for naming the Panama Canal designed by American engineers, or the airplane developed by the Wright Brothers, or the automobile, mentioning either the gas engine developed by Daimler and Benz, or the assembly line developed by Ford.

Learning Coach Guide
Lesson 1: The Great War Begins

Nationalism, military alliances, and a large degree of overconfidence sparked the First World War. Could the nations of the world face off against each other and fight a short war? The thinking was "Can do!" The result was a disaster.

Lesson Objectives

- Recognize the term "the Great War" was used at the time to describe World War I.
- Recognize the slogans "make the world safe for democracy" and "the war to end all wars" as slogans that brought the United States into World War I.
- Describe World War I as a long and deadly war involving many nations and great destruction.
- Explain that trench warfare was characteristic of World War I.
- Explain that American entry into World War I turned the tide of victory.
- Explain that the peace that followed the war left many people dissatisfied.
- Describe the Russian Revolution as one that involved the overthrow of the czar and the triumph of Communism.
- Describe the 1920s in the United States as a period of economic growth and many social changes.
- Describe the Great Depression as a world-wide economic depression in the 1930s.
- Name some of the key figures of the period from 1914 to 1930 (Woodrow Wilson, Vladmir Lenin, Josef Stalin, Alice Paul, Charles Lindbergh, Alexander Fleming, Franklin Delano Roosevelt).
- Name some of the key events, phrases, and advances of the period between 1914 and 1930 (World War I, League of Nations, Russian Revolution, Roaring Twenties, women's suffrage, solo flight across the Atlantic, discovery of penicillin, the Great Depression).
- Explain that nationalism and military alliances triggered the First World War.
- Explain that advances in technology contributed to a long and deadly war.
- Describe the nations of Europe as confident that the war would be short.
- State that the "the Great War" was the term used to describe World War I.

PREPARE

Approximate lesson time is 60 minutes.

Materials

For the Student

- Map of Europe on the eve of World War I, 1914
- Alliances

Keywords and Pronunciation

alliance (uh-LIY-uhnts) : An agreement between partners; an agreement between countries to help each other.

TEACH

Activity 1: The Powder Keg of Europe *(Online)*

Instructions

This main teaching activity is online. Your student may complete this activity alone or with your help.

Activity 2: History Journal *(Offline)*

Instructions

With your student, read the History Journal entry for today's lesson and compare it with the sample paragraph below. Did it include the most important parts of the lesson?

World War I was a horrible war that many nations fought. Nationalism was one reason for the war. Many nations in Europe thought they were better than everyone else. They made alliances with other nations. They promised to fight with each other against enemies. Before long, many nations were fighting each other. Everyone thought the war would be short, but scientists made new weapons such as tanks and airplanes. The war lasted a long time. Back then, people called it the Great War. We call it World War I.

Activity 3: Alliances *(Offline)*

Instructions

Have the student complete the Alliances activity sheet.

Answers:

1. The Allies
2. Central Powers
3. Balkans
4. Great War; long

ASSESS

Lesson Assessment: The Great War Begins (*Online*)

Students will complete an online assessment based on the lesson objectives. The assessment will be scored by the computer. The attached answer key is the most current and may not coincide with previously printed guides.

Learning Coach Guide
Lesson 2: In Flanders Fields

A terrible war raged for four years on two fronts. Soldiers experienced the horrors of trench warfare, poison gas attacks, lice, disease, and death. One Canadian doctor wrote a famous poem expressing hope that they would not die in vain.

Lesson Objectives

- Explain that the Great War became a very long and deadly war.
- Describe World War I as fought on eastern and western fronts.
- Name two characteristics of trench warfare on the western front.
- Explain that the poem "In Flanders Fields" expressed the hope that the soldiers would not die in vain.

PREPARE

Approximate lesson time is 60 minutes.

Materials

For the Student

📖 Map of Europe on the eve of World War I, 1914

📖 The Tragedy of War

Keywords and Pronunciation

front : In war, a line of battle; an area where enemy armies face each other.

John McCrae (muh-KRAY)

trench : A long cut in the ground; a ditch.

TEACH
Activity 1: A Long War *(Online)*
Instructions

This main teaching activity is online. Your student may complete this activity alone or with your help.

Activity 2: History Journal *(Offline)*
Instructions

With your student, read the History Journal entry for today's lesson and compare it with the sample paragraph below. Did it include the most important parts of the lesson?

The Great War was a long war. Many people got hurt and were killed. Soldiers fought on the eastern front and the western front. On the western front, they dug many trenches. Soldiers lived in the trenches. It was dirty and muddy living there, but the trenches helped protect the soldiers from bullets. One soldier wrote a poem called "In Flanders Fields." Many people thought it was a beautiful poem. It was very sad. It said that the soldiers should not have to die in vain.

Activity 3: A Long and Deadly War *(Offline)*
Instructions
Have the student make a bar graph to compare casualties from the Great War with those from previous wars.

ASSESS

Lesson Assessment: In Flanders Fields (*Online*)
Students will complete an online assessment based on the lesson objectives. The assessment will be scored by the computer. The attached answer key is the most current and may not coincide with previously printed guides.

Learning Coach Guide
Lesson 3: Lafayette, We Are Here!

The United States had a history of isolationism. But angered by German attacks on civilians, the U.S. entered WWI in 1917. American manpower and technology turned the tide of war for the Allies, and the United States was a world power by the close of the war.

Lesson Objectives

- Explain that since Washington's Farewell Address, the United States had stayed out of European wars.
- Identify Woodrow Wilson as president of the United States during World War I.
- Recognize that "make the world safe for democracy" was a United States slogan in World War I and a reason for entering the war.
- State that the arrival of U.S. troops in Europe helped the Allies begin to win the war.

PREPARE

Approximate lesson time is 60 minutes.

Materials

For the Student

📖 Americans Over There

poster board

Keywords and Pronunciation

Saint-Nazaire (sen-nah-ZEHR)

TEACH
Activity 1: Americans Over There *(Online)*
Instructions

This main teaching activity is online. Your student may complete this activity alone or with your help.

Activity 2: History Journal *(Offline)*
Instructions

With your student, read the History Journal entry for today's lesson and compare it with the sample paragraph below. Did it include the most important parts of the lesson?

The United States sent many men and machines to fight in World War I. The United States had stayed out of Europe's wars for a long time. George Washington had told Americans to stay out. But German submarines began attacking American ships. Woodrow Wilson was now president. He said America must help fight the Germans. He said that America must help make the world safe for democracy. The American troops helped win the war for the Allies.

Activity 3: Newspaper Headlines *(Offline)*
Instructions
Have your student create a poster of newspaper headlines from the Great War. The following are some examples. These come from the first half of the lesson.

Wilson Leads U.S. Into War

U.S. Troops Arrive In France

U.S. Troop Ships Avoid U-Boats In Atlantic

America Joins Allies To Make World Safe For Democracy

ASSESS
Lesson Assessment: Lafayette, We Are Here! (*Online*)
Students will complete an online assessment based on the lesson objectives. The assessment will be scored by the computer. The attached answer key is the most current and may not coincide with previously printed guides.

TEACH
Activity 4. Optional: Lafayette, We Are Here! *(Offline)*
Instructions
Have your student do some research on the Marquis de Lafayette to find out why Americans respect him so much. He should use a variety of reference materials to learn about his role in the American Revolution.

Learning Coach Guide
Lesson 4: Dashed Hopes

World War I had begun in an age of optimism. It ended with near despair: millions dead and billions spent, infrastructures ruined, nations bankrupted, and some nations (such as Russia) in revolution. Woodrow Wilson proposed a League of Nations to head off future wars. But the peace treaties the nations signed made Germany resentful and left much business unfinished in Europe.

Lesson Objectives

- Explain that World War I ended on November 11, 1918, and that that day is remembered as Veterans Day in the U.S.
- Name two terrible results of World War I (such as millions dead; economies ruined; factories, roads, railroads, and buildings destroyed; anger and resentment on all sides).
- Explain that Woodrow Wilson proposed the League of Nations to stop future wars, and that the United States did not join the League.
- Recognize that the peace treaty blamed Germany for the war and demanded reparations.

PREPARE

Approximate lesson time is 60 minutes.

Materials

For the Student

- 📖 Map of Europe after World War I, 1920
- 📖 Ratifying a Treaty

Keywords and Pronunciation

reparation : Repairs; payment for damages.

TEACH
Activity 1: A War to End All Wars? *(Online)*

Instructions

This main teaching activity is online. Your student may complete this activity alone or with your help.

Activity 2: History Journal *(Offline)*

Instructions

With your student, read the History Journal entry for today's lesson and compare it with the sample paragraph below. Did it include the most important parts of the lesson?

World War I finally ended on November 11, 1918. Today we call that day Veterans Day. The countries of Europe were wrecked at the end of the war. Factories and roads were destroyed. The peace treaty blamed Germany for the war and said it must make reparations. Woodrow Wilson wanted a League of Nations after the war, but the United States did not join. So even though the war was over, people were still sad and angry.

Activity 3: Ratifying a Treaty *(Offline)*
Instructions
Have your student read the Ratifying a Treaty activity sheet. He should then write a short paragraph in his History Journal explaining what a treaty is and how a treaty in the United States is ratified.

ASSESS

Lesson Assessment: Dashed Hopes (*Online*)
Students will complete an online assessment based on the lesson objectives. The assessment will be scored by the computer. The attached answer key is the most current and may not coincide with previously printed guides.

Learning Coach Guide
Lesson 5: Russia's Czar Dethroned and Lenin Rising

World War I brought much hardship to the Russian people. By the end of the war, they were struggling to survive and weary of the iron rule of the czars. Revolution brought Lenin and his Communist Party to power. Would life for the Russian peasants improve at last?

Lesson Objectives

- Name two hardships suffered by the Russian people in World War I (such as lack of housing; not enough food; not enough fuel to keep warm; many soldiers killed).
- State that revolutionaries overthrew the Russian Czar.
- Describe Lenin as an admirer of Marx's ideas and the founder of the Communist Party in Russia.
- Explain that Lenin ruled Russia as a Communist dictator.

PREPARE

Approximate lesson time is 60 minutes.

Materials

For the Student

📖 Map of Europe after World War I, 1920

Keywords and Pronunciation

Bolsheviks (BOHL-shuh-viks)

dictator (DIK tay tur) : A ruler with absolute power.

soviet : A council.

Vladimir Ilyich Ulyanov (vluh-DYEEM-yir il-YEECH ool-YAH-nef)

TEACH
Activity 1: The Bolsheviks Rule Russia *(Online)*
Instructions
This main teaching activity is online. Your student may complete this activity alone or with your help.

Activity 2: Report from Russia *(Offline)*
Instructions
Have the student write a news article about the overthrow of the Russian Czar and the rise to power of the Communist Party.

The following is a model article you can use to check the student's work.

Russians revolt!

The Russian people have long suffered many hardships. Czars have ruled Russia with an iron hand for hundreds of years. Conditions worsened during the Great War. Many Russians, both soldiers and civilians, died during the war. Many people did not have enough to eat. The peasants wanted land and bread.

At the beginning of 1917, the czar was overthrown in a revolution. A new democratic government took power. But little changed. Workers and peasants were still hungry. They had no land. The war with Germany continued.

A political party organized at this time. The Bolsheviks believed in the teachings of Karl Marx. They thought money and land should be taken away from the rich and divided among the people. Their leader was Vladimir Lenin. Lenin, a Communist, had read books by Karl Marx.

In October 1917, the Bolsheviks rose up against the government. Under the leadership of Lenin, they quickly took over and set up a new government. He ordered land to be taken away from rich landowners and given to the peasants. He changed the name of the Bolshevik Party to the Communist Party.

Soon Lenin ruled as a communist dictator. The Communist Party began to arrest people who stood in its way. Russians have no more freedom than they had under the czars. Hardships for the Russian people continue under the Communist government.

ASSESS

Lesson Assessment: Russia's Czar Dethroned and Lenin Rising (*Offline*)

Students will complete an offline assessment based on the lesson objectives. Print the assessment and have students complete it on their own. Use the answer key to score the assessment, and then enter the results online. The attached answer key is the most current and may not coincide with previously printed guides.

Lesson Assessment Answer Key

Russia's Czar Dethroned and Lenin Rising

Answers:

1. Answers should include any two of the following hardships:
   lack of housing
   not enough food
   not enough fuel to keep warm
   many soldiers killed.

2. Czar

3. Marx; Communist

4. Lenin; dictator

Learning Coach Guide
Lesson 6: From Lenin to Stalin

Russia's Communist Party triumphed in a two-year civil war. It brought several neighboring areas under communist rule. The new nation was named the Union of Soviet Socialist Republics, or the U.S.S.R. Joseph Stalin succeeded Lenin as a ruthless Communist dictator.

Lesson Objectives

- Explain that after a civil war in Russia, the Communist Party controlled the country.
- Explain that during the war, the Communist army was called the Red Army because of the color of its flag.
- State that after the Communists triumphed, they named their country the Soviet Union, or U.S.S.R.
- Describe Joseph Stalin as a powerful and ruthless dictator who followed Lenin.

PREPARE

Approximate lesson time is 60 minutes.

Materials

For the Student

📖 A Changing Russia

Keywords and Pronunciation

dictator (DIK tay tur) : A ruler with absolute power.
Joseph Stalin (JOH-zuhf STAH-luhn)
Siberia (siy-BIHR-ee-uh)

TEACH
Activity 1: Stalinist Russia (Online)

Instructions

This main teaching activity is online. Your student may complete this activity alone or with your help.

Activity 2: History Journal (Offline)

Instructions

With your student, read the History Journal entry for today's lesson and compare it with the sample paragraph below. Did it include the most important parts of the lesson?

Joseph Stalin was a brutal dictator of the Soviet Union. He got power after a terrible civil war in Russia. The Communist Party and the Red Army won the civil war. After that, Russia became the Soviet Union. Stalin told farmers in the Soviet Union that they had to grow more food. When they could not grow enough food, he had many people killed. People were very scared of Stalin. He was a cruel ruler.

Activity 3: A Changing Russia *(Offline)*

Instructions

Have your student complete the A Changing Russia activity sheet.

Answers:

1. Correct order: C, A, D, F, E, B

   Russia's new name: Union of Soviet Socialist Republics

   Shortened to: the Soviet Union

   Initials: U.S.S.R.

2. The Communist army was called the Red Army because their flag was red.

3. Stalin's rule can best be described as harsh, ruthless, and cruel. He was one of the cruelest rulers in history. He used terror to turn the Soviet Union into a major industrial and military power.

ASSESS

Lesson Assessment: From Lenin to Stalin *(Online)*

Students will complete an online assessment based on the lesson objectives. The assessment will be scored by the computer. The attached answer key is the most current and may not coincide with previously printed guides.

Learning Coach Guide
Lesson 7: American Women Get the Vote

In the early 1900s, more and more people said it was ridiculous that women couldn't vote. The woman's suffrage movement pressed hard for change. By 1920 the 19th Amendment to the Constitution guaranteed that right.

Lesson Objectives

- Define *suffrage* as the right to vote.
- Describe the woman's suffrage movement as the movement for the right of women to vote.
- Identify Alice Paul as a leader in the woman's suffrage movement.
- Explain that an amendment to the U.S. Constitution gave women the right to vote.

PREPARE

Approximate lesson time is 60 minutes.

Materials

For the Student

History Journal

Keywords and Pronunciation

picketer : Someone who protests outside a building.

Suffrage : The right to vote.

Suffragist : In this lesson, someone who supports the right of women to vote.

TEACH
Activity 1: A Lady with a Mission *(Online)*

Instructions

This teaching activity is online. Your student may want to complete this activity by himself, or you may want to join him at the computer as he reads how women fought for the right to vote.

Activity 2: History Journal *(Offline)*

Instructions

With your student, read the History Journal entry for today's lesson and compare it with the sample paragraph below. Did it include the most important parts of the lesson?

Women worked hard to get suffrage in America. Suffrage is the right to vote. For a long time, many women in the United States were not allowed to vote. Women like Alice Paul said that was not right. Alice Paul, a leader in the suffrage movement, wanted an amendment to the Constitution. She kept asking President Woodrow Wilson for the right to vote. She sent women to stand outside the White House with protest signs. Finally Congress passed the 19th Amendment. Then all women had the right to vote in America.

Activity 3: Time to Protest (Offline)

Instructions

Have your student make a poster that could have been carried in the Washington, D.C. suffrage parade.

ASSESS

Lesson Assessment: American Women Get the Vote (Online)

Students will complete an online assessment based on the lesson objectives. The assessment will be scored by the computer. The attached answer key is the most current and may not coincide with previously printed guides.

Learning Coach Guide
Lesson 8: The Roaring '20s

A booming economy and a lively social scene in the cities made the 1920s "the Roaring Twenties." Numerous new inventions--from radios and automobiles to jazz, dance, and movies--made the decade exciting.

Lesson Objectives

- Explain that in the United States, the 1920s was a decade of good times.
- Associate the phrase "Roaring 20s" with the 1920s.
- Name some new forms of entertainment that Americans enjoyed in the 20s, such as jazz, the Charleston, radio.

PREPARE

Approximate lesson time is 60 minutes.

Materials

For the Student

History Journal

🖳 Vocabulary of the Roaring 20s

TEACH
Activity 1: A Decade of Good Times *(Online)*

Instructions

This main teaching activity is online. Your student may want to complete this activity by himself, or you may want to join him at the computer as he reads about a young woman's exciting new life in the big city during the Roaring Twenties.

Activity 2: History Journal *(Offline)*

Instructions

You will use the student's History Journal entry to assess his understanding of this lesson. Compare it with the sample paragraph below. Did he include, in some way, the following:

- The decade of the 1920s in the United States was a period of good (exciting) times.
- The 1920s are called the Roaring 20s.
- Some of the new forms of entertainment that Americans enjoyed in the 20s included: dancing (the Charleston), listening to the radio, listening to jazz, sitting on flagpoles, and cutting their hair short.

The 1920s are called the Roaring 20s. Many people were having a good time. Many people moved to cities to find jobs. They made money and had fun doing things like dancing and listening to the radio. They did a new dance called the Charleston. They listened to jazz. Women liked to cut their hair short. They were called flappers. People did crazy things like sitting on flagpoles. The Roaring 20s were an exciting time.

Activity 3: Vocabulary of the Roaring 20s *(Offline)*
Instructions
Have your student complete an activity sheet to reinforce the vocabulary of the Roaring 20s. Check his work.

Answers:
1. Businesses often paid flagpole sitters to sit atop flagpoles as publicity stunts.
2. Most flapper girls wore there hair very short. This style was called a bob.
3. Flapper girls liked to try all the new fads - short hair, short dresses, fast autos, and fast dances.
4. jazz
5. Charleston
6. Answers may vary. Bee knees means "excellent - the highest quality." Its origin comes from the bee. Bees carry pollen back to their hives in sacs on their legs. The phrase refers to the concentrated goodness that's found around the bee's knees.

Activity 4. Optional: The Roaring '20s *(Offline)*
Instructions
Help your student learn how to do the Charleston. Step by step directions and diagrams, along with a sample of Charleston music, can be found at: http://lancefuhrer.com/charleston.htm.

ASSESS
Lesson Assessment: The Roaring '20s (*Online*)
Use the answer key to evaluate your students' essay and input the total point value in the assessment. The attached answer key is the most current and may not coincide with previously printed guides.

Lesson Assessment Answer Key

The Roaring '20s

Answers:

Answers will vary. Use the following grading rubric to award points for this question:

Did your student include, in some way, the fact that in the United States, the 1920s was a decade of good times? *(10 points)*	
Did your student include, in some way, the fact that the phrase "Roaring 20s" refers to the decade of the 1920s? *(10 points)*	
Did your student include, in some way, the fact that some of the new forms of entertainment that Americans enjoyed in the 20s included: doing the Charleston, listening to the radio, listening to jazz, sitting on flagpoles, and wearing short hair? *(10 points)*	
Total *(30 points max)*:	

Learning Coach Guide
Lesson 9: Charles Lindbergh and Advances in Flight

In his plane, the *Spirit of St. Louis,* Charles Lindbergh was the first person to fly solo across the Atlantic Ocean. His feat inspired millions and encouraged further advances in aviation.

Lesson Objectives

- Describe Charles Lindbergh as the first man to fly solo across the Atlantic Ocean.
- Identify Lindbergh's plane as the *Spirit of St. Louis.*
- Explain that Charles Lindbergh became a hero.
- Explain that Lindbergh used his fame to encourage further work in aviation.

PREPARE

Approximate lesson time is 60 minutes.

Keywords and Pronunciation
aviation : The science of flying; air travel.

TEACH
Activity 1: Lucky Lindy Makes the Hop *(Online)*
Instructions
This main teaching activity is online. Your student may complete this activity alone or with your help.

Activity 2: History Journal *(Offline)*
Instructions
With your student, read the History Journal entry for today's lesson and compare it with the sample paragraph below. Did it include the most important parts of the lesson?

Charles Lindbergh was the first person to fly alone across the Atlantic Ocean. Other people had tried, but they did not make it. Lindbergh called his plane the *Spirit of St. Louis.* He flew from New York to Paris. It was a long flight. It got very cold. He had to sing to himself to stay awake. Finally he saw land. He flew until he came to the airport in Paris. People called him Lucky Lindy. He was a great hero. Because of Lindbergh, other people wanted to fly, too.

Activity 3: The Spirit of St. Louis Award *(Offline)*
Instructions
Your student will create an award to be given to people who--like Charles Lindbergh did--advance aviation in some way.

ASSESS
Lesson Assessment: Charles Lindbergh and Advances in Flight (*Online*)
Students will complete an online assessment based on the lesson objectives. The assessment will be scored by the computer. The attached answer key is the most current and may not coincide with previously printed guides.

TEACH
Activity 4. Optional: Charles Lindbergh and Advances in Flight (*Online*)
Instructions
Have your student draw a map of Lindbergh's flight from New York to Paris. He'll then use a timeline from the Charles Lindbergh: An American Aviator website to plot significant points along the route.

Learning Coach Guide
Lesson 10: Fleming and Penicillin: Advances in Medicine

Following Louis Pasteur's discovery that some bacteria cause diseases, scientists began to search for a way to kill harmful bacteria. The answer finally came when British scientist Alexander Fleming discovered penicillin, a wonder drug and the first antibiotic.

Lesson Objectives

- Describe antibiotics as drugs that fight harmful bacteria.
- Identify penicillin as the first antibiotic drug.
- Describe penicillin as a powerful antibiotic capable of curing many diseases.
- Identify Alexander Fleming as the British scientist who discovered penicillin.

PREPARE

Approximate lesson time is 60 minutes.

Materials

For the Student

History Journal

📖 The Vocabulary of Antibiotics

Breakthrough: The True Story of Penicillin by Francine Jacobs

Keywords and Pronunciation

antibiotic : A drug made from live microbes that kills harmful bacteria.

bacteria : a kind of microscopic organism.

germs : The common name for disease-causing bacteria.

microbe (MIY-krohb) : A name for any microscopic organism.

Penicillium notatum (pen-ih-SIL-ee-uhm noh-TAH-toum)

Staphylococcus (STA-fuh-loh-KAH-kuhs)

TEACH
Activity 1: Penicillin--The First Antibiotic *(Online)*
Instructions

This main teaching activity is online. Your student may complete this activity alone or with your help.

Activity 2: History Journal *(Offline)*
Instructions

You will use your student's History Journal entry as the lesson assessment.

Answers:

In 1928 a scientist in London made an important discovery. He was looking for a way to kill harmful bacteria. His name was **Alexander Fleming**. He discovered that a certain mold killed harmful staphylococcus germs. His discovery led to the development of **penicillin**, the first antibiotic drug. Antibiotics are **drugs** that fight harmful **bacteria**. Penicillin is a powerful **antibiotic** capable of curing many **diseases.**

Activity 3: The Vocabulary of Antibiotics *(Offline)*

Instructions
Have your student print and complete The Vocabulary of Antibiotics activity sheet.

ASSESS

Lesson Assessment: Fleming and Penicillin: Advances in Medicine (*Online*)
Use the answer key to evaluate your students' History Journal entry and input the total point value in the assessment. The attached answer key is the most current and may not coincide with previously printed guides.

TEACH

Activity 4. Optional: Fleming and Penicillin: Advances in Medicine *(Offline)*

Instructions
Check your library or local bookstore for *Breakthrough: The True Story of Penicillin* by Francine Jacobs (Putnam Publishing Group, 1985).

Name _____ Date _____

Lesson Assessment Answer Key

Fleming and Penicillin: Advances in Medicine

Answers:

Award 7 points for each correct answer (42 points max).

In 1928 a scientist in London made an important discovery. He was looking for a way to kill harmful bacteria. His name was **Alexander Fleming**. He discovered that a certain mold killed harmful staphylococcus germs. His discovery led to the development of **penicillin**, the first antibiotic drug. Antibiotics are **drugs** that fight harmful **bacteria**. Penicillin is a powerful **antibiotic** capable of curing many **diseases**.

Learning Coach Guide
Lesson 11: The Great Depression

During the Great Depression, thousands of banks, stores, and factories closed and millions of people were out of work worldwide. In the United States, Franklin Delano Roosevelt had ideas for change. He proved to be the right man for hard times.

Lesson Objectives

- Describe the Great Depression as a time when many banks, stores, and factories closed, and many people lost their jobs.
- Identify Franklin Delano Roosevelt as president of the United States during the Great Depression.
- Explain that Roosevelt started the New Deal, government programs to help get people back to work and give them hope.

PREPARE

Approximate lesson time is 60 minutes.

Keywords and Pronunciation

depression : A time when the economy is very bad; a time when businesses, factories, and stores close, and many people lose their jobs.

Franklin Delano Roosevelt (DEL-uh-noh ROH-zuh-velt)

TEACH
Activity 1: Looking for a Few Good Jobs *(Online)*
Instructions
This main teaching activity is online. Your student may complete this activity alone or with your help.

Activity 2: History Journal *(Offline)*
Instructions
With your student, read the History Journal entry for today's lesson and compare it with the sample paragraph below. Did it include the most important parts of the lesson?

The Great Depression was a very hard time. Many people lost their jobs. Some people had to move out of their houses and go look for new jobs. Some families lived in tents. Franklin Delano Roosevelt was the president during the Great Depression. He had a plan called the New Deal. The government gave jobs to people. They did things like build dams and plant trees. Some people got jobs, but the Great Depression was very bad.

Activity 3: A Little Research (Offline)
Instructions
Have your student do some research on a topic related to today's lesson.

ASSESS
Lesson Assessment: The Great Depression (Offline)
Students will complete an online assessment based on the lesson objectives. The assessment will be scored by the computer. The attached answer key is the most current and may not coincide with previously printed guides.

TEACH
Activity 4. Optional: The Great Depression (Online)
Instructions
Have your student explore some more of Roosevelt's New Deal or interview someone who remembers the Great Depression.

National Association of Civilian Conservation Corps Legacy website is a good source of information.

Learning Coach Guide
Lesson 12: Unit Review and Assessment

The student will review this unit and take the unit assessment.

Lesson Objectives

- Demonstrate mastery of important knowledge and skills in this unit.
- Explain that the Great War became a very long and deadly war.
- Name two characteristics of trench warfare on the western front.
- Identify Woodrow Wilson as president of the United States during World War I.
- Recognize that "make the world safe for democracy" was a United States slogan in World War I and a reason for entering the war.
- State that the arrival of U.S. troops in Europe helped the Allies begin to win the war.
- Name two terrible results of World War I (such as millions dead; economies ruined; factories, roads, railroads, and buildings destroyed; anger and resentment on all sides).
- Explain that Woodrow Wilson proposed the League of Nations to stop future wars, and that the United States did not join the League.
- Recognize that the peace treaty blamed Germany for the war and demanded reparations.
- Explain that after a civil war in Russia, the Communist Party controlled the country.
- Describe Joseph Stalin as a powerful and ruthless dictator who followed Lenin.
- Describe the woman's suffrage movement as the movement for the right of women to vote.
- Identify Alice Paul as a leader in the woman's suffrage movement.
- Explain that in the United States, the 1920s was a decade of good times.
- Name some new forms of entertainment that Americans enjoyed in the 20s, such as jazz, the Charleston, radio.
- Describe Charles Lindbergh as the first man to fly solo across the Atlantic Ocean.
- Identify Lindbergh's plane as the *Spirit of St. Louis.*
- Identify penicillin as the first antibiotic drug.
- Identify Alexander Fleming as the British scientist who discovered penicillin.
- Describe the Great Depression as a time when many banks, stores, and factories closed, and many people lost their jobs.
- Identify Franklin Delano Roosevelt as president of the United States during the Great Depression.
- Explain that Roosevelt started the New Deal, government programs to help get people back to work and give them hope.
- Describe Lenin as an admirer of Marx's ideas and the founder of the Communist Party in Russia.

PREPARE

Approximate lesson time is 60 minutes.

TEACH
Activity 1: Mostly Hard Times: War, the Roaring 20s, and Depression (Offline)
Instructions
The student will review this unit and take the unit assessment.

Activity 2: History Journal Review (Offline)
Instructions
The student will use the History Journal to review for the unit assessment. You can help by asking questions based on the work in the journal.

Activity 3: Online Interactive Review (Online)
Instructions
The student will continue reviewing the unit by completing an online, interactive review.

ASSESS
Unit Assessment: Mostly Hard Times: War, the Roaring 20s, and Depression (Offline)
Students will complete an offline Unit Assessment. Print the assessment and have students complete it on their own. Use the answer key to score the assessment, and then enter the results online. The attached answer key is the most current and may not coincide with previously printed guides.

Mostly Hard Times

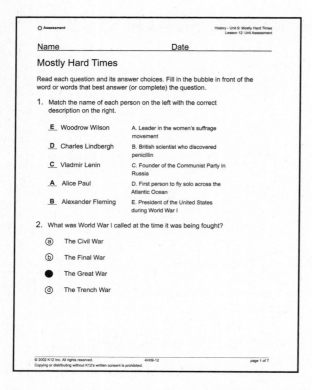

Name _____   Date _____

Mostly Hard Times

Read each question and its answer choices. Fill in the bubble in front of the word or words that best answer (or complete) the question.

1. Match the name of each person on the left with the correct description on the right.

   E Woodrow Wilson — A. Leader in the women's suffrage movement

   D Charles Lindbergh — B. British scientist who discovered penicillin

   C Vladmir Lenin — C. Founder of the Communist Party in Russia

   A Alice Paul — D. First person to fly solo across the Atlantic Ocean

   B Alexander Fleming — E. President of the United States during World War I

2. What was World War I called at the time it was being fought?

   ⓐ The Civil War

   ⓑ The Final War

   ● The Great War

   ⓓ The Trench War

---

3. Which of the following was an American slogan during World War I—and a reason for entering the war?

   ⓐ "We have nothing to fear but fear itself!"

   ⓑ "Take up our quarrel with the foe!"

   ⓒ "The people need land! The people need bread!"

   ● "Make the world safe for democracy!"

4. What did the peace treaty that ended World War I say about Germany?

   ⓐ Germany should take large parts of France and get reparations from England.

   ● Germany was to blame for the war and should pay reparations.

   ⓒ Germany should pay back the Ottoman Turks and remove the Kaiser.

   ⓓ Germany was to keep a large army and police Europe.

---

5. Which of the following was NOT true at the end of World War I?

   ⓐ Millions of people had been killed or wounded.

   ⓑ There was a lot of anger and resentment in many countries.

   ● People were hopeful and convinced it was the last war.

   ⓓ Many factories, roads, and buildings were destroyed.

6. At the end of World War I, Woodrow Wilson proposed an organization to help nations get together to talk and sort things out. What was it called?

   ● The League of Nations

   ⓑ The New Deal Nations

   ⓒ The Council of Nations

   ⓓ The Union of Nations

7. During the Russian Revolution, the people of Russia overthrew their czar. What replaced the czar?

   ⓐ The Democratic party

   ● The Communist party

   ⓒ The Soviet Council

   ⓓ The Suffragist movement

---

8. After Lenin, who ruled the Soviet Union as a ruthless dictator?

   ⓐ Kaiser Wilhelm

   ⓑ John McCrae

   ⓒ Nicholas II

   ● Joseph Stalin

9. In the United States, why were the 1920s known as the Roaring Twenties?

   ● The country roared with a good economy and good times.

   ⓑ The country seemed to be roaring toward another world war.

   ⓒ The country roared along with Franklin Roosevelt's New Deal.

   ⓓ The country could hear the Great War roaring in Europe.

10. What did women gain from the women's suffrage movement?

   ⓐ The right to free speech

   ⓑ The right to protest

   ⓒ The right to work

   ● The right to vote

Mostly Hard Times

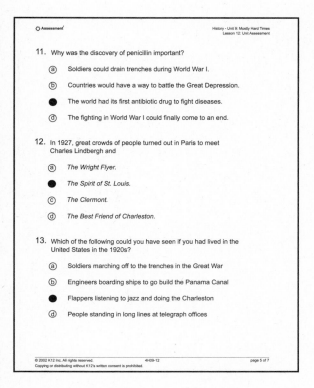

11. Why was the discovery of penicillin important?

    (a) Soldiers could drain trenches during World War I.

    (b) Countries would have a way to battle the Great Depression.

    ● The world had its first antibiotic drug to fight diseases.

    (d) The fighting in World War I could finally come to an end.

12. In 1927, great crowds of people turned out in Paris to meet Charles Lindbergh and

    (a) *The Wright Flyer.*

    ● *The Spirit of St. Louis.*

    (c) *The Clermont.*

    (d) *The Best Friend of Charleston.*

13. Which of the following could you have seen if you had lived in the United States in the 1920s?

    (a) Soldiers marching off to the trenches in the Great War

    (b) Engineers boarding ships to go build the Panama Canal

    ● Flappers listening to jazz and doing the Charleston

    (d) People standing in long lines at telegraph offices

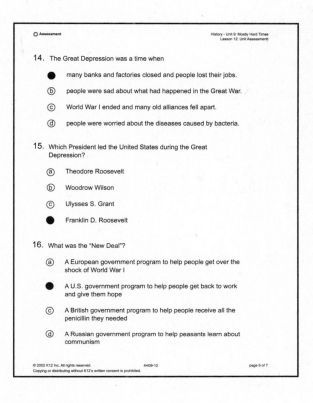

14. The Great Depression was a time when

    ● many banks and factories closed and people lost their jobs.

    (b) people were sad about what had happened in the Great War.

    (c) World War I ended and many old alliances fell apart.

    (d) people were worried about the diseases caused by bacteria.

15. Which President led the United States during the Great Depression?

    (a) Theodore Roosevelt

    (b) Woodrow Wilson

    (c) Ulysses S. Grant

    ● Franklin D. Roosevelt

16. What was the "New Deal"?

    (a) A European government program to help people get over the shock of World War I

    ● A U.S. government program to help people get back to work and give them hope

    (c) A British government program to help people receive all the penicillin they needed

    (d) A Russian government program to help peasants learn about communism

17. Put the following events in chronological order.

    (a) Roaring 20s, Russian Revolution, World War I

    (b) World War I, Great Depression, Roaring 20s

    ● World War I, Roaring 20s, Great Depression

    (d) Great Depression, World War I, Russian Revolution

18. Essay Question

Write a paragraph about World War I. Start with the topic sentence: When World War I began, many people thought it would be a short, easy war.

Include the following:
- Tell whether the World War I turned out to be a long, deadly war or a short, easy war.
- Explain what *trench warfare* was, and describe life in the trenches.
- Tell how the arrival of U.S. troops in Europe affected the war.

_____
_____
_____
_____
_____
_____
_____
_____
_____

Scoring the Essay Question

This essay question is worth forty points. Score the student's writing as follows:

- Ten points for stating that the war turned out to be a long, deadly war.
- Ten points for explaining that "trench warfare" meant that soldiers often lived in and fought from trenches they dug.
- Ten points for including any of the following: Life in the trenches was hard. Soldiers could not get dry or clean. The trenches were usually dirty. They often had rats, disease, and lice. When it rained, water poured into the trenches. The soldiers fired at the enemy from their trenches.
- Ten points for explaining that the arrival of U.S. troops helped the Allies win the war.

Learning Coach Guide
Lesson 1: The Rise of Dictators

The Great Depression affected the whole world. People suffered, and they turned to strong--and often evil--leaders who promised order and prosperity. Nations with no democratic tradition, such as the Soviet Union, Italy, Germany, and Japan, became dictatorships in the 1930s.

Lesson Objectives

- Recognize that in the years after World War I, many nations turned to dictators as leaders.
- Explain that Germany, Italy and Japan attempted to invade and conquer their neighbors.
- Explain that Hitler attempted to conquer large parts of Europe and describe "appeasement" as the Allied response.
- State that Germany, Italy, and Japan fought as the "Axis" powers in World War II, and that Great Britain, the United States, and the Soviet Union fought as the "Allies."
- Define the terms appeasement and blitzkrieg.
- Describe the Holocaust as the Nazi attempt to kill the world's Jews in concentration camps.
- Describe the significance of key events and battles of World War II (Hitler's invasion of Poland, the Battle of Britain, the Holocaust, Pearl Harbor, D-Day, Hiroshima, V-J Day).
- Identify major world leaders during World War II and the countries they led: Hitler, Mussolini, Stalin, Churchill, Franklin Roosevelt, Dwight Eisenhower, Harry Truman.
- Describe the triumph of the Allied powers in World War II as the triumph of democracy over the dictators.
- Explain that World War I left many problems unsolved and the Great Depression affected the whole world.
- Explain that during the Great Depression people were looking for strong leaders who promised order and prosperity.
- Identify Stalin, Hitler, and Mussolini as dictators who led the Soviet Union, Germany, and Italy.
- State that the Japanese were led by a military dictatorship.

PREPARE

Approximate lesson time is 60 minutes.

Materials

For the Student

- Map of Europe on the Eve of World War II
  map, world
- How Could it Happen?

Keywords and Pronunciation

Benito Mussolini (beh-NEE-toh moos-soh-LEE-nee)

dictator (DIK tay tur) : A ruler with absolute power.

TEACH

Activity 1: Strong Leaders Who Promised Much *(Online)*

Instructions

This main teaching activity is online. Your student may want to complete this activity by herself, or you may want to join her at the computer as she reads about the rise of dictators.

Activity 2: History Journal *(Offline)*

Instructions

With your student, read the History Journal entry for today's lesson and compare it with the sample paragraph below. Did it include the most important parts of the lesson?

Countries had many problems after World War I. Many people had been killed. People were out of work, too. They were looking for strong leaders who said they could fix things. Dictators took power. Stalin ruled in the Soviet Union. Mussolini ruled in Italy. Hitler came to power in Germany. Army leaders ruled Japan. These dictators were strong, but many people thought they were dangerous.

Activity 3: How Could it Happen? *(Offline)*

Instructions

Have your student print and complete the How Could it Happen activity sheet. Check her completed work. Answers:

1. Answers could include: many people had been killed in World War I; economies had been ruined; factories, roads, and buildings had been destroyed; some countries had lost territories; German people did not think the peace settlement was fair; the Great Depression had caused factories to close and people to lose jobs.

2. Answers could include: the dictator has all the power; the only laws that matter are the ones the dictator likes; people have to give up their rights and freedom; no one is allowed to say what he or she thinks; everyone has to do what the dictator wants.

3. Answers could include: restore country to greatness (Mussolini); build new empires (Mussolini); avenge defeat in World War I (Hitler); make Germany proud and pure again (Hitler); improve industry and farms (Stalin); became a great power in Asia (Japan).

4. Accept any reasonable answer.

ASSESS

Lesson Assessment: The Rise of Dictators *(Offline)*

Students will complete an offline assessment based on the lesson objectives. Print the assessment and have students complete it on their own. Use the answer key to score the assessment, and then enter the results online. The attached answer key is the most current and may not coincide with previously printed guides.

Lesson Assessment Answer Key

The Rise of Dictators

Answers:

1. False

2. False

3. strong leaders

4. dictators (or military dictators)

5. __B__ Joseph Stalin
   __C__ Adolph Hitler
   __A__ Benito Mussolini

6. military dictators

Learning Coach Guide
Lesson 2: Hitler's Gamble

In the 1930s Japan, Italy, and Germany began to invade other nations. They gambled that the other countries of the world were not ready to fight another war. Hitler posed the biggest threat of all. He invaded the Rhineland, annexed Austria, snatched up the Sudetenland, and then took all of Czechoslovakia.

Lesson Objectives
- Explain that Japan, Italy, and Germany began to invade other nations.
- Describe Hitler as the greatest threat to peace and name two areas he conquered.
- Define *appease* and describe *appeasement* as the Allied policy of letting Hitler have what he wanted, hoping it would prolong peace.

PREPARE

Approximate lesson time is 60 minutes.

Materials
For the Student
- Europe on the Eve of WWII

  History Journal
- Europe Appeases Hitler
- Map of Europe on the Eve of World War II

Keywords and Pronunciation
appease : To make peace with someone by giving that person whatever he wants.
Czechoslovakia (cheh-kuh-sloh-VAH-kee-uh)
Sieg heil (zeek hiyl)
Sudetenland (soo-DAY-tun-land)

TEACH
Activity 1: Germany Reaches for Empire *(Online)*
Instructions
This main teaching activity is online. Your student may want to complete this activity by herself, or you may want to join her at the computer as she reads about Hitler's bold gamble.

Activity 2: History Journal *(Offline)*
Instructions
With your student, read the History Journal entry for today's lesson and compare it with the sample paragraph below. Did it include the most important parts of the lesson?

Germany, Japan, and Italy began to invade other countries. They did not think other nations would do anything about it. Hitler invaded the Rhineland and the Sudetenland. He took Austria, too. The Allies tried to appease Hitler. They let him invade other nations because they did not want to fight him. Hitler just wanted more and more, though.

Activity 3: Europe Appeases Hitler *(Offline)*
Instructions
Have your student print and complete the Europe Appeases Hitler activity sheet. Check his completed work.

Part of the activity sheet will be used to assess your student's understanding of today's lesson.

ASSESS

Lesson Assessment: Hitler's Gamble (*Offline*)
Review your student's responses on the Europe Appeases Hitler activity sheet and input the results online.

The attached answer key is the most current and may not coincide with previously printed guides.

Lesson Assessment Answer Key

Hitler's Gamble

Answers:

1. Italy; Germany; Japan

2. Hitler

3. *Any two of the following are acceptable:*
   the Rhineland; Austria; Czechoslovakia; the Sudetenland

4. to make peace with someone by giving him what he wants

5. The Allies' policy of appeasement was to let Hitler have what he wanted in the hope that it would prolong peace.

Learning Coach Guide
Lesson 3: Nazi Blitzkrieg and Axis Expansion

World War II began on September 1, 1939 when Germany invaded Poland. Germany's *blitzkrieg* quickly brought much of Europe under Nazi rule. The Italians battered the British in North Africa, and the Japanese pressed into China and Southeast Asia.

Lesson Objectives
- Explain that when Hitler attacked Poland, Great Britain and France declared war on Germany.
- Explain that the world plunged into a second terrible war called World War II.
- Define *blitzkrieg* as "lightning war" and explain that it was a German attack strategy involving speed and surprise.
- Explain that much of Europe, including France, fell to Hitler during the German *blitzkrieg*.

PREPARE

Approximate lesson time is 60 minutes.

Materials
For the Student
- Hitler's Blitz
- Map of Europe during World War II
- History Journal

Keywords and Pronunciation
blitzkrieg (BLITS-kreeg) : A new kind of warfare conducted with great speed and force.
Champs-Élysées (shawn-zay-lee-ZAY)
newsreel : A short movie dealing with current events.

TEACH
Activity 1: Europe Erupts *(Online)*

Instructions
This main teaching activity is online. Your student may want to complete this activity by herself, or you may want to join her at the computer as she reads about the Nazi *blitzkrieg*.

Activity 2: History Journal *(Offline)*

Instructions
With your student, read the History Journal entry for today's lesson and compare it with the sample paragraph below. Did it include the most important parts of the lesson?
Hitler launched *blitzkrieg* attacks on much of Europe. *Blitzkrieg* means lighting war. Hitler used it to surprise other countries. He attacked Poland. Then Great Britain and France decided to declare war on Germany. Hitler marched across Europe. He even attacked France and captured Paris. Hitler's *blitzkrieg* atttacks defeated many countries in Europe.

Activity 3: Hitler's Blitz *(Offline)*
Instructions
Have your student print and complete the Hitler's Blitz activity sheet.

ASSESS

Lesson Assessment: Nazi Blitzkrieg and Axis Expansion (*Online*)

Students will complete an online assessment based on the lesson objectives. The assessment will be scored by the computer. The attached answer key is the most current and may not coincide with previously printed guides.

Learning Coach Guide
Lesson 4: Churchill Leads Embattled Britain

After France surrendered, Hitler planned to invade England. The Germans began to bomb London in preparation. But Hitler hadn't counted on Winston Churchill, the Royal Air Force, and British resolve.

Lesson Objectives

- Identify Winston Churchill as the prime minister of Great Britain during World War II.
- Explain that in the Battle of Britain, the Nazis launched air attacks on London and were defeated by the Royal Air Force.
- Explain that Churchill led Great Britain through the Battle of Britain.
- State that Hitler invaded the Soviet Union, widening the war to the east.

PREPARE

Approximate lesson time is 60 minutes.

TEACH
Activity 1: Britain Stands Alone *(Online)*
Instructions

This main teaching activity is online. Your student may want to complete this activity by herself, or you may want to join her at the computer as she reads how Churchill leads embattled Britain.

Activity 2: Letter for Help *(Offline)*
Instructions

Have your student write a letter to a relatives asking if her children can stay with the relatives in the countryside during the Battle of Britain.

The following paragraph is a sample and can be used as a model to check your student's work.

Summer, 1940

Dear Father,

The situation in London is grave. Hitler is sending hundreds of bombers to attack London. This evil man is a threat to Great Britain. He has already conquered most of Europe. He's not worried about the Soviet Union because he has signed a treaty with them. So now he has turned his greedy eyes toward our country.

Our Royal Air Force is fighting gallantly. They rise each time to meet the bombers. Our pilots are brave men. Winston Churchill, who as you know is our prime minister, is leading our nation through this battle. Speaking about our brave pilots, he told the country that "never in the field of human conflict was so much owed by so many to so few."

But it's still dangerous in the city. We would like to send your grandchildren to live with you in the country until the danger has passed.

Your son,

John

ASSESS

Lesson Assessment: Churchill Leads Embattled Britain (*Online*)

Students will complete an online assessment based on the lesson objectives. The assessment will be scored by the computer. The attached answer key is the most current and may not coincide with previously printed guides.

Learning Coach Guide
Lesson 5: The Holocaust

Hitler blamed Germany's problems on the Jews and began to persecute them early on. His "final solution" was to round up millions of Jews for labor and death in concentration camps. The Holocaust refers to the murder of millions of Jews in World War II. The story of Anne Frank shows us courage and determination in unspeakably difficult times.

Lesson Objectives

- Explain that Hitler blamed Germany's problems on the Jews.
- Describe the Holocaust as the mass murder of millions of Jews by the Nazis.
- Explain that concentration camps were places where many Jews were taken, tortured and killed.
- Explain that Anne Frank was a Jewish girl who hid with her family.

PREPARE

Approximate lesson time is 60 minutes.

Materials

For the Student

History Journal

📖 Anne Frank activity sheet

Keywords and Pronunciation

Holocaust : The mass murder of millions of Jews in World War II.

TEACH
Activity 1: Anne Frank's Story (Online)
Instructions

This main teaching activity is online. Your student may want to complete this activity by herself, or you may want to join her at the computer as she reads about the Holocaust.

Activity 2: History Journal (Offline)
Instructions

With your student, read the History Journal entry for today's lesson and compare it with the sample paragraph below. Did it include the most important parts of the lesson?

Hitler and the Nazis killed millions of Jews during the Holocaust. Hitler blamed the Jews for Germany's problems. He arrested Jews and sent them to concentration camps. The Jews had to work like slaves in the camps. The Nazis murdered many Jews there. Some Jews hid from the Nazis. Anne Frank and her family found a hiding place. Anne Frank was very brave during the Holocaust.

Activity 3: Anne Frank (Offline)

Instructions

Your student will print and complete the Anne Frank activity sheet.

Answers:

1. the Jews
2. places where many Jews were taken, tortured, and killed
3. the Holocaust
4. Anne Frank

ASSESS

Lesson Assessment: The Holocaust (Online)

Students will complete an online assessment based on the lesson objectives. The assessment will be scored by the computer. The attached answer key is the most current and may not coincide with previously printed guides.

TEACH

Activity 4. Optional: The Holocaust (Online)

Instructions

With your student, explore the Anne Frank Online website at Anne Frank Online.

Learning Coach Guide
Lesson 6: Pearl Harbor and United States Entry into the War

Americans were reluctant to enter World War II until December 7, 1941, when Japan launched a surprise attack on the U.S. naval base at Pearl Harbor. U.S. President Franklin Roosevelt called it "a date which will live in infamy," and the United States declared war on the Axis powers.

Lesson Objectives

- Explain that the Japanese launched a surprise attack on the U.S. Naval Base at Pearl Harbor in Hawaii on December 7, 1941.
- Recognize the phrase "a date which will live in infamy" as the words President Roosevelt used to describe the attack on Pearl Harbor.
- Explain that the attack on Pearl Harbor brought the United States into World War II.

PREPARE

Approximate lesson time is 60 minutes.

Materials

For the Student

map, world

History Journal

⌨ A Date Which Will Live in Infamy activity sheet

Keywords and Pronunciation

infamy : A reputation for evil.

TEACH
Activity 1: Japan's Expanding Empire (Online)
Instructions

This main teaching activity is online. Your student may want to complete this activity by herself, or you may want to join her at the computer as she reads about Pearl Harbor and U.S. entry into the war.

Activity 2: History Journal (Offline)
Instructions

With your student, read the History Journal entry for today's lesson and compare it with the sample paragraph below. Did it include the most important parts of the lesson?

Many Americans did not want the United States to get into World War II. Pearl Harbor changed that. The Japanese made a surprise attack against the U.S. navy base at Pearl Harbor. President Roosevelt said that December 7, 1941, was "a date which will live in infamy." After Pearl Harbor, the United States began to fight in World War II.

Activity 3: A Date Which Will Live in Infamy *(Offline)*
Instructions
Have your student print and complete the A Date Which Will Live in Infamy activity sheet.

Answers:
1. Answers will vary but should indicate that before the attack on Pearl Harbor, the two nations were at peace and were trying to maintain peace in the Pacific.
2. No. The Japanese ambassador to the U.S. delivered a message that contained no hint or threat of war.
3. Yes. The Japanese ambassador delivered that message one hour after the attack began. Because of the great distance between Japan and the United States, the attack had to have been planned several days or weeks before the message was delivered.
4. Answers will vary. Americans were surprised and shocked by the attack because the Japanese government deceived the United States with lies. The Japanese were expressing hopes for continued peace.

ASSESS

Lesson Assessment: Pearl Harbor and United States Entry into the War
(Online)

Students will complete an online assessment based on the lesson objectives. The assessment will be scored by the computer. The attached answer key is the most current and may not coincide with previously printed guides.

TEACH

Activity 4. Optional: Pearl Harbor and United States Entry into the War *(Online)*
Instructions
Explore with your student National Geographic's website on Pearl Harbor at
http://channel.nationalgeographic.com/episode/attack-on-pearl-harbor-3037.

Learning Coach Guide
Lesson 7: D-Day and Victory in Europe

Hitler's forces had rolled across much of Europe, but the Allies fought back. With the United States in the war, the Allies launched an invasion of Europe. D-Day, led by General Dwight D. Eisenhower, turned the tide of the war.

Lesson Objectives

- Explain that D-Day was the day of a huge Allied invasion of France from across the English Channel.
- Name Dwight D. Eisenhower as the commander of the Allied invasion force.
- Recognize that the Allies suffered great losses on D-Day, but that the invasion turned the tide of the war.
- State that Germany surrendered to the Allies in 1945.

PREPARE

Approximate lesson time is 60 minutes.

Materials

For the Student
- Map of Europe during World War II
- History Journal
- From England to Berlin

Lesson Notes

The character Frank in this story is a fictional charcter.

Keywords and Pronunciation

Bergen-Belsen (BEHR-guhn-BEL-zuhn)

Buchenwald (BOO-kuhn-vahlt)

Calais (ka-LAY)

Champs-Élysées (shawn-zay-lee-ZAY)

Dwight D. Eisenhower (dwiyt dee IYZ-uhn-how-ur)

TEACH
Activity 1: Invading Nazi Europe *(Online)*

Instructions

This main teaching activity is online. Your student may want to complete this activity by herself, or you may want to join her at the computer as she reads about D-Day and victory in Europe.

Activity 2: History Journal (Offline)

Instructions

With your student, read the History Journal entry for today's lesson and compare it with the sample paragraph below. Did it include the most important parts of the lesson?

D-Day was June 6, 1944. The Allies carried out a huge invasion that day. Dwight D. Eisenhower was the commander of the attack. The Allies crossed the English Channel in lots of ships. They landed on the beaches in France and fought the Germans. Many soldiers were killed, but the Allies won. Eventually the Allies got France back. Germany surrendered, and the Allies won World War II.

Activity 3: From England to Berlin (Offline)

Instructions

Have your student print and complete the From England to Berlin activity sheet. Check her work.

Answers:

4. D-Day

5. Dwight D. Eisenhower

9. Buchenwald and Bergen-Belsen

10. May 1945

ASSESS

Lesson Assessment: D-Day and Victory in Europe (Online)

Students will complete an online assessment based on the lesson objectives. The assessment will be scored by the computer. The attached answer key is the most current and may not coincide with previously printed guides.

TEACH

Activity 4. Optional: D-Day and Victory in Europe (Online)

Instructions

Explore with your student some websites that are dedicated to D-Day and the Allied invasion at Normandy.

Learning Coach Guide
Lesson 8: The Atomic Bomb and V-J Day

After the United States dropped the atomic bomb on the Japanese cities of Hiroshima and Nagasaki, Japan surrendered. World War II came to an end. But an atomic age began.

Lesson Objectives

- Describe the atomic bomb as an incredibly powerful bomb developed secretly in the United States during World War II.
- Explain that the United States used the atomic bomb on Hiroshima and Nagasaki to end the war.
- Name some of the effects of the bomb, such as whole cities destroyed, many people killed, sickness from radiation.
- State that the Japanese surrendered shortly after the bombing of Nagasaki.

PREPARE

Approximate lesson time is 60 minutes.

Materials

For the Student
- Map of Pacific Theater, 1945
- History Journal
- War in the Pacific Ends

Keywords and Pronunciation

Hiroshima (hee-roh-SHEE-mah)
Nagasaki (nah-gah-SAH-kee)
uranium (yoo-RAY-nee-uhm)

TEACH
Activity 1: Victory in the Pacific (Online)
Instructions

This main teaching activity is online. Your student may want to complete this activity by herself, or you may want to join her at the computer as she reads about the victory in the Pacific.

Activity 2: History Journal (Offline)
Instructions

With your student, read the History Journal entry for today's lesson and compare it with the sample paragraph below. Did it include the most important parts of the lesson?

The United States used the atomic bomb to defeat the Japanese in World War II. The atomic bomb was a terrible new weapon. The United States dropped the bomb on Hiroshima and Nagasaki. Many people were killed. Many buildings were destroyed. The Japanese knew they had to surrender. World War II was finally over.

Activity 3: War in the Pacific Ends (Offline)

Instructions

Have your student print and complete the War in the Pacific Ends activity sheet. Check her work.

Answers:

6. Acceptable answers include powerful, strong, or deadly; secretly (or in secret), or quickly; World War II

8. The effects of the atomic bomb include: whole cities were destroyed; many people were killed; people became sick from the radiation.

9. surrendered

ASSESS

Lesson Assessment: The Atomic Bomb and V-J Day (Online)

Students will complete an online assessment based on the lesson objectives. The assessment will be scored by the computer. The attached answer key is the most current and may not coincide with previously printed guides.

Learning Coach Guide
Lesson 9: Unit Review and Assessment

The student will review this unit and take the unit assessment.

Lesson Objectives

- Demonstrate mastery of important knowledge and skills in this unit.
- Identify Winston Churchill as the prime minister of Great Britain during World War II.
- Identify Stalin, Hitler, and Mussolini as dictators who led the Soviet Union, Germany, and Italy.
- Define *appease* and describe *appeasement* as the Allied policy of letting Hitler have what he wanted, hoping it would prolong peace.
- Explain that when Hitler attacked Poland, Great Britain and France declared war on Germany.
- Define *blitzkrieg* as "lightning war" and explain that it was a German attack strategy involving speed and surprise.
- Explain that in the Battle of Britain, the Nazis launched air attacks on London and were defeated by the Royal Air Force.
- Describe the Holocaust as the mass murder of millions of Jews by the Nazis.
- Explain that Anne Frank was a Jewish girl who hid with her family.
- Explain that the Japanese launched a surprise attack on the U.S. Naval Base at Pearl Harbor in Hawaii on December 7, 1941.
- Recognize the phrase "a date which will live in infamy" as the words President Roosevelt used to describe the attack on Pearl Harbor.
- Explain that the attack on Pearl Harbor brought the United States into World War II.
- Explain that D-Day was the day of a huge Allied invasion of France from across the English Channel.
- Name Dwight D. Eisenhower as the commander of the Allied invasion force.
- Explain that the United States used the atomic bomb on Hiroshima and Nagasaki to end the war.
- State that the Japanese surrendered shortly after the bombing of Nagasaki.
- Recognize that in the years after World War I, many nations turned to dictators as leaders.
- State that Germany, Italy, and Japan fought as the "Axis" powers in World War II, and that Great Britain, the United States, and the Soviet Union fought as the "Allies."

PREPARE

Approximate lesson time is 60 minutes.

TEACH
Activity 1: World War II *(Offline)*
Instructions
The student will review this unit and take the unit assessment.

Activity 2: History Journal Review *(Offline)*
Instructions
The student will use the History Journal to review for the unit assessment. You can help by asking questions based on the work in the journal.

Activity 3: Online Interactive Review *(Online)*
Instructions
The student will continue reviewing the unit by completing an online, interactive review.

ASSESS
Unit Assessment: World War II (*Offline*)
Students will complete an offline Unit Assessment. Print the assessment and have students complete it on their own. Use the answer key to score the assessment, and then enter the results online. The attached answer key is the most current and may not coincide with previously printed guides.

World War II

Name _____ Date _____

World War II

Read each question and its answer choices. Fill in the bubble in front of the word or words that best answer (or complete) the question.

1. Match the name of the person on the left with a description of the country he led during World War II on the right.

   _D_ Adolf Hitler   **A.** Soviet Union

   _E_ Benito Mussolini   **B.** United States

   _A_ Joseph Stalin   **C.** Great Britain

   _C_ Winston Churchill   **D.** Germany

   _B_ Franklin D. Roosevelt **E.** Italy

2. Why did dictators come to power in Europe and Japan in the years following World War I?

   (a) People wanted strong leaders to keep complex alliances in place.

   (b) People wanted dictators to end the Industrial Revolution for good.

   ● People were looking for strong leaders who promised better times.

   (d) People wanted dictators to make sure no single country grew too strong.

3. When Adolf Hitler began taking over territories in Europe, Great Britain and France responded with a policy of appeasement. In other words, they

   (a) tried to keep peace by making Hitler pull his army back.

   (b) began building up their armies and making loud threats.

   (c) began taking over more territories of their own in Europe.

   ● tried to keep peace by giving Hitler whatever he wanted.

4. What was the name of Adolf Hitler's political party?

   (a) The Red Shirts

   ● The Nazi Party

   (c) The Communist Party

   (d) The Axis Party

5. What did Great Britain and France do when Adolf Hitler attacked Poland, his neighbor to the east?

   (a) They decided to look the other way again, hoping to avoid a war.

   ● They finally declared war on Germany, and World War II began.

   (c) They asked the League of Nations to order an end to the attacks.

   (d) They made Germany agree to pay large reparations for the invasion.

6. Hitler used *blitzkrieg* at the outset of World War II. What was *blitzkrieg*?

   (a) False war, using threats and empty promises

   (b) Trench war, using a long series of trenches

   ● Lightning war, using speed and surprise

   (d) Bombing war, using attacks from the air

7. For Americans, December 7 is known as "Pearl Harbor Day" because of the events of December 7, 1941. How did President Franklin D. Roosevelt describe that day?

   (a) "Our country's darkest hour"

   (b) "The day the whole earth stood still"

   (c) "Our country's finest hour"

   ● "A date which will live in infamy"

8. Germany, Italy, and Japan were known as the _____ powers during World War II, and Great Britain, France, the United States, and the Soviet Union were known as the _____ powers.

   ● Axis; Allied

   (b) Allied; Axis

   (c) Central; Allied

   (d) Allied; Central

9. During World War II, many British parents in London and other big cities decided to send their children to the countryside. Why did they do that?

   (a) Diseases were sweeping the big cities, and there was a shortage of penicillin.

   (b) German armies had crossed the English Channel and were invading big cities.

   ● The Germans were launching air attacks on cities during the Battle of Britain.

   (d) Children worked in factories in the countryside to help build British airplanes.

10. What was D-Day?

    ● The day the Allies launched an invasion of France across the English Channel.

    (b) The day Germany surrendered, bringing an end to World War II in Europe.

    (c) The day Japan surrendered, bringing an end to World War II in the Pacific.

    (d) The day Germany launched an invasion of Europe and triggered World War II.

World War II

11. Who was Dwight D. Eisenhower?

    ⓐ The American president who made the decision to drop the atomic bomb.

    ⓑ The British prime minister who led his country during its darkest hour.

    ⓒ The British general who insisted that Hitler must be stopped, regardless of the cost.

    ● The American commander who led the invasion of Europe from Great Britain.

12. As the Allies pushed toward Germany, they saw evidence of one of the greatest horrors of World War II. Today we remember it as the Holocaust. What was the Holocaust?

    ⓐ The bombing of German cities by British and American war planes

    ● The mass murder of millions of Jews by the Nazis

    ⓒ The starvation of millions of Russians on the orders of Joseph Stalin

    ⓓ The destruction of cities by Adolf Hitler's armies

13. Anne Frank is now one of the most famous names of World War II. This Jewish girl showed courage and hope while doing which of the following?

    ● Hiding from the Nazis with her family

    ⓑ Fighting the Germans as a French soldier

    ⓒ Serving as a spy in the Netherlands

    ⓓ Escaping from a Nazi concentration camp

14. Who became President after Franklin Roosevelt and made the decision to drop the atomic bomb?

    ⓐ Dwight D. Eisenhower

    ⓑ George Marshall

    ● Harry Truman

    ⓓ Woodrow Wilson

15. On which two cities did the United States drop atomic bombs during World War II?

    ⓐ Tokyo and Hiroshima

    ⓑ Berlin and Tokyo

    ● Hiroshima and Nagasaki

    ⓓ Berlin and Moscow

16. What happened after the United States used the atomic bomb in World War II?

    ⓐ Germany and Japan formed a new alliance against the United States.

    ● Japan surrendered, bringing an end to the war in the Pacific.

    ⓒ Japan fought back, causing the war to drag on for months.

    ⓓ Germany and the Soviet Union both surrendered to the United States.

17. Essay Question

Write a brief essay about Pearl Harbor. Start with this topic sentence:
Americans will long remember the events of December 7, 1941.

Include the following:
• Tell where Pearl Harbor is located.
• Describe what the Japanese did at Pearl Harbor.
• Tell what the United States did after the events at Pearl Harbor.

_____
_____
_____
_____
_____
_____
_____
_____
_____

Scoring the Essay Question

This essay question is worth fifty points. Score the student's writing as follows:

• Ten points for stating that Pearl Harbor is in Hawaii.
• Twenty points for explaining that the Japanese attacked American ships at Pearl Harbor.
• Twenty points for explaining that after the attack on Pearl Harbor, the United States entered World War II, or declared war on Japan.

Learning Coach Guide
Lesson 1: Lending a Hand with the Marshall Plan

Mindful of the consequences of economic devastation after the First World War, the United States proposed to end the Second World War differently. The victors proposed a bold plan--the Marshall Plan--to feed and rebuild the war-torn nations.

Lesson Objectives

- Describe some ways nations attempted to rebuild a better world after World War II and identify some of the people who worked for these changes (Marshall Plan, formation of the United Nations, Declaration of Universal Human Rights, Harry Truman, George Marshall, Eleanor Roosevelt).
- Explain that after the second world war many colonial empires collapsed and name Ghandi as the leader of Indian independence.
- Describe the Cold War as a post-war struggle between the United States and the Soviet Union, between democratic and communist nations.
- Identify the build up of nuclear weapons as the greatest fear and threat to peace.
- Identify some of the key figures, symbols, and events of the Cold War (Stalin, Truman, Mao Ze Dong, John F. Kennedy, the Berlin Wall, Ronald Reagan).
- Explain that the post-war period was a time of advance in medicine and technology and name some of these advances (such as polio vaccine, lunar landing and space travel).
- Explain that the Cold War ended and the Soviet Union collapsed in 1989 when the Berlin Wall fell.
- Describe Europe as a continent in ruins at the end of the Second World War.
- Explain that Harry Truman thought the best chance for lasting peace was to help war-torn nations rebuild with sound economies and democratic governments.
- Describe the Marshall Plan as the U.S. plan to help rebuild Europe.
- Recognize that the Marshall Plan was named after Secretary of State George Marshall.

PREPARE

Approximate lesson time is 60 minutes.

TEACH
Activity 1: Rebuilding Europe (Online)
Instructions

This main teaching activity is online. Your student may complete this activity alone or with your help.

Activity 2: Introducing the Marshall Plan (Offline)

Instructions

Your student will imagine that he is Marshall's speechwriter and write a speech that Marshall would have given to Congress.

ASSESS

Lesson Assessment: Lending a Hand with the Marshall Plan (Online)

Students will complete an online assessment based on the lesson objectives. The assessment will be scored by the computer. The attached answer key is the most current and may not coincide with previously printed guides.

Learning Coach Guide
Lesson 2: Formation of the United Nations

Seeing the failed attempts to promote international cooperation after World War I, victor nations hoped for better results after World War II. They came together to form the United Nations (UN), a forum in which nearly 160 nations could discuss problems. The UN is officially dedicated to the promotion of world peace and dignity.

Lesson Objectives

- Describe the United Nations as an international organization formed to promote world peace.
- Explain that the UN was founded at the end of World War II to encourage cooperation among nations.
- Explain that the UN's Universal Declaration of Human Rights spelled out rights for people all over the world.
- Name Eleanor Roosevelt as the person who led the effort to write the Universal Declaration of Human Rights.

PREPARE

Approximate lesson time is 60 minutes.

Materials

For the Student

    🖥 The United Nations

Keywords and Pronunciation

commission : A group of people who are given a duty to perform.

TEACH
Activity 1: Eleanor Roosevelt and Human Rights *(Online)*
Instructions

The main teaching activity is online. Your student may complete this activity alone or with your help.

Activity 2: History Journal *(Offline)*
Instructions

Read the paragraph your student wrote about the United Nations in his History Journal. Compare it with the following paragraph. You will use this paragraph to assess the student's understanding of this lesson.
The United Nations is an international organization that was formed at the end of World War II. It was created to promote world peace and encourage cooperation among nations. The United Nations' Universal Declaration of Human Rights is a document that lists 30 rights that every person should have. Eleanor Roosevelt led the effort to write this document.

Activity 3: The United Nations (Offline)

Instructions

Have your student print and complete the United Nations activity sheet.

ASSESS

Lesson Assessment: Formation of the United Nations (Online)

Review your student's responses in the History Journal entry and input the results online. The attached answer key is the most current and may not coincide with previously printed guides.

Lesson Assessment Answer Key

Formation of the United Nations

Answers:

1. The United Nations is an international organization and was created to promote world peace.

2. The United Nations was founded at the end of World War II.

3. The United Nation's Universal Declaration of Human Rights is a document that lists rights that every person should have.

4. Eleanor Roosevelt was the person who led the effort to write the Universal Declaration of Human Rights.

Learning Coach Guide
Lesson 3: End of Empires: Gandhi in India

Colonial empires would never be the same after World War II. The Indian independence movement, spearheaded by Mohandas Gandhi, led the way. Considered the father of the Indian nation, Gandhi used nonviolent resistance to win India's independence from Great Britain.

Lesson Objectives

- Explain that India had been ruled by Great Britain.
- Identify Mohandas Gandhi as the leader of the movement for Indian independence.
- Explain that Gandhi used peaceful resistance to oppose British rule, and give one example of that technique (such as fasting, the Salt March, or wearing Indian cloth instead of British cloth).
- Explain that after World War II, European colonial empires began to disappear.

PREPARE

Approximate lesson time is 60 minutes.

Materials
    For the Student
        globe

Keywords and Pronunciation
Dandi (dahn-dee)

khadi (kah-dee)

Mohandas Gandhi (MOH-huhn-dahs GAHN-dee)

TEACH
Activity 1: The Nonviolent Fight for Indian Independence (Online)
Instructions
This main teaching activity is online. Your student may complete this activity alone or with your help.

Activity 2: Gandhi Opposes British Rule (Offline)
Instructions
Have your student write two paragraphs explaining how Gandhi helped India win its independence from Britain without firing a shot. In his first paragraph, he should explain how Gandhi used peaceful resistance to gain Indian independence. In the second paragraph, he should explain why he thinks peaceful resistance worked.

Use the following paragraph as a model to check your student's work.

Mohandas Gandhi helped India gain independence. He worked for independence using peace. Some examples of peaceful resistance he used are 1) he led the Salt March to show that Indians should be able to make their own salt, 2) he and other Indians wore clothes made from Indian cloth instead of British cloth, and 3) he and other Indians fasted.

Finally India got its freedom after World War II. Peaceful resistance had worked. The British, who had fought for democracy during the war, finally understood what Gandhi had been saying all along. The British could not live up to their own ideals of freedom and equality while they ruled over India.

ASSESS

Lesson Assessment: End of Empires: Gandhi in India (*Online*)

Students will complete an online assessment based on the lesson objectives. The assessment will be scored by the computer. The attached answer key is the most current and may not coincide with previously printed guides.

TEACH

Activity 3. Optional: End of Empires: Gandhi in India (*Offline*)

Instructions

Help your student compare the American and Indian drives for independence.

The following are two similarities:

- Both Indian and American colonists stopped importing British cloth and made clothes using homespun cloth. (George Washington made a point of wearing it at his inauguration.)
- The Indians marched to the sea to make salt in defiance of British laws that prohibited Indians from making their own salt. It was a symbolic gesture of resistance. In the same way, the American colonists refused to drink British tea, choosing instead to dump it into Boston harbor. Theirs was also a symbolic gesture of resistance against the mother country.

Learning Coach Guide
Lesson 4: The Cold War and the Berlin Wall

Although the "hot war" against the Axis powers had ended, a Cold War seemed to have begun between two new superpowers, the United States and the Soviet Union. Americans worried about the Iron Curtain the Soviets had drawn over Eastern Europe. Within Eastern Europe, people still struggled for freedom and self-rule.

Lesson Objectives

- Describe the Cold War as a dangerous period of rivalry between the United States and the Soviet Union.
- Explain that as chief rivals in the Cold War, the Soviet Union led communist nations and the United States led democratic nations.
- Explain that each side built nuclear weapons, which implied the threat of a third world war.
- Explain that the Berlin Wall was a wall erected by communists to keep people in East Berlin.

PREPARE

Approximate lesson time is 60 minutes.

Materials

For the Student
Optional

- 🖥 Map of Europe
- 🖥 Geography of the Cold War
- 🖥 Map of Cold War Europe, 1962

The Fall of the Berlin Wall: The Cold War Ends by Nigel Kelly

Keywords and Pronunciation

Czechoslovakia (cheh-kuh-sloh-VAH-kee-uh)

TEACH
Activity 1: A War and a Wall (Online)
Instructions
This main teaching activity is online. Your student may complete this activity alone or with your help.

Activity 2: History Journal (Offline)
Instructions
With your student, read the History Journal entry for today's lesson and compare it with the sample paragraph below. Did it include the most important parts of the lesson?

The Cold War came after World War II. The Soviet Union led the communist countries. The United States led democracies. Both sides built nuclear weapons. People were afraid of another world war. The communists built the Berlin Wall to keep people from escaping East Berlin. The Cold War was a very dangerous time.

Activity 3: Geography of the Cold War *(Offline)*
Instructions
Have your student print and complete the Geography of the Cold War activity sheet. Check his work.

Answers:
1. the Cold War
2. nuclear (or atomic)
3. democratic; communist
4. American Allies: West Germany, France, England, Austria
   Under Soviet Influence: East Germany, Poland, Czechoslovakia, Hungary
5. They built a wall.

ASSESS
Lesson Assessment: The Cold War and the Berlin Wall *(Online)*
Students will complete an online assessment based on the lesson objectives. The assessment will be scored by the computer. The attached answer key is the most current and may not coincide with previously printed guides.

TEACH
Activity 4. Optional: The Cold War and the Berlin Wall *(Offline)*
Instructions
For a look ahead, check your library or local bookstore for *The Fall of the Berlin Wall: The Cold War Ends,* by Nigel Kelly (Heinemann Library, 2001).

The fall of the Berlin Wall will be covered in a lesson at the end of this unit.

Learning Coach Guide
Lesson 5: Mao Zedong in China

One of the most famous faces in the world, Mao Zedong (or Mao), made China a Communist nation in 1949. Mao kept a tight control over Chinese society, using his Great Cultural Revolution to silence intellectual opposition.

Lesson Objectives

- Describe Mao Zedong as the leader who made China a Communist nation.
- Describe Mao's tight control over China.
- Explain that the Cultural Revolution was an attempt to silence those who did not agree with Mao's ideas.

PREPARE

Approximate lesson time is 60 minutes.

Materials

> For the Student
>
> > globe
> >
> > 🖥 Mao's Ever Present Face

Keywords and Pronunciation

Hu Meiping (hoo may-ping)
Mao Zedong (maou dzuh-doung)
Zhang Sing-Nan (jahng shing-ahn)

TEACH
Activity 1: Chairman Mao (Online)
Instructions

This main teaching activity is online. Your student may complete this activity alone or with your help.

Activity 2: History Journal (Offline)
Instructions

With your student, read the History Journal entry for today's lesson and compare it with the sample paragraph below. Did it include the most important parts of the lesson?

China turned into a Communist country. Its leader was Mao Zedong. Mao controlled how the Chinese people lived. He told them they had to work harder. He said they had to agree with his ideas. Mao arrested people who were enemies of communism. He sent them to jail. This was called the Great Cultural Revolution.

Activity 3: Mao's Ever Present Face *(Offline)*
Instructions
Have your student print and complete the Mao's Ever Present Face activity sheet. Check his work.

Answers:

1. False. Mao was born into a peasant family. It is true, however, that he grew up to be a revolutionary.
2. True
3. False. Mao was the leader who made China a Communist nation.
4. False. The Red Guard was an army of loyal youth that Mao used against the enemies of true communism. Members of the Red Guard often spied on their neighbors. The Red Guard was part of Chairman Mao's Great Cultural Revolution.
5. True
6. True

ASSESS

Lesson Assessment: Mao Zedong in China (*Online*)
Students will complete an online assessment based on the lesson objectives. The assessment will be scored by the computer. The attached answer key is the most current and may not coincide with previously printed guides.

Learning Coach Guide
Lesson 6: Defeating Polio

Great epidemics of polio spread around the world. The disease that crippled Franklin Delano Roosevelt was feared everywhere. In the 1950s American scientist Jonas Salk introduced a vaccine that prevented polio and ended the spread of this dreaded disease.

Lesson Objectives

- Describe polio as a disease that struck thousands of people every year.
- Describe polio as a disease that paralyzed or crippled many of its victims.
- Identify Jonas Salk as the creator of a vaccine to prevent polio.
- Explain that polio ceased to be a threat when the vaccine was given in childhood.

PREPARE

Approximate lesson time is 60 minutes.

Materials

> For the Student
>> Jonas Salk and the Polio Vaccine by John Bankston

Keywords and Pronunciation

epidemic : An outbreak of disease among many people.

virus : Microscopic organisms that cause diseases.

TEACH
Activity 1: The Cure for Polio (*Online*)

Instructions

This main teaching activity is online. Your student may want to complete this activity by himself, or you may want to join him at the computer as he reads about the cure for polio.

Activity 2: Polio Vaccine Invented! (*Offline*)

Instructions

Have your student write a newspaper article reporting the invention of the polio vaccine. You will use his article as today's lesson assessment.

ASSESS

Lesson Assessment: Defeating Polio (*Online*)

Use the answer key to evaluate your students' essay and input the total point value in the assessment. The attached answer key is the most current and may not coincide with previously printed guides.

TEACH
Activity 3. Optional: Defeating Polio *(Offline)*
Instructions
Check your library or local bookstore for *Jonas Salk and the Polio Vaccine*, by John Bankston (Mitchell Lane Publishers, 2001).

Lesson Assessment Answer Key

Defeating Polio

Answers:

Answers will vary. Use the following grading rubric to award points for this question:

Did your student's article include the fact that polio is a disease that affected thousands of people every year? *(10 points)*	
Did your student's article include the fact that polio paralyzed or crippled many of its victims? *(10 points)*	
Did your student's article include the fact that Jonas Salk was the creator of the vaccine that prevents polio? *(10 points)*	
Did your student's article include the fact that polio stopped being a threat when the vaccine was given in childhood? *(10 points)*	
Total *(40 points max)*:	

Learning Coach Guide
Lesson 7. Optional: A Computer Revolution

We think of the computer revolution as a modern phenomenon. But the history leading to computers is a long one, going back hundreds of years to the beginnings of the Scientific Revolution. Today we learn about some machines that are considered "ancestors" of the computer.

Lesson Objectives

- Recognize that scientists and mathematicians have been building machines to help them calculate and solve problems for hundreds of years.
- Explain that in the twentieth century powerful computers that can store large amounts of information and do complex calculations quickly were developed.
- Give an example of how computers help people solve problems or communicate faster than ever before.

PREPARE

Approximate lesson time is 60 minutes.

Keywords and Pronunciation

Blaise Pascal (blez pahs-KAHL)

census : A count of the population.

Colossus (kuh-LAH-suhs)

compute : To make calculations

Joseph-Marie Jacquard (zhoh-zef ma-REE zhah-kahr)

Pascaline (PA-skuh-liyn)

UNIVAC (YOO-nih-vac)

TEACH
Activity 1. Optional: Optional Lesson Instructions *(Online)*

Activity 2. Optional: A Computer Family Album *(Online)*

Instructions

This main teaching activity is online. Your student may complete this activity alone or with your help.

Note: A simulated computer error occurs in this lesson. It is designed to look realistic but there is no cause for alarm. It is harmless and instructions are provided to your student on how to proceed.

Activity 3. Optional: History Journal *(Offline)*
Instructions
With your student, read the History Journal entry for today's lesson and compare it with the sample paragraph below. Did it include the most important parts of the lesson?

Scientists have been building machines to help them add, subtract, and solve problems for hundreds of years. For example, in 1642 a French mathematician named Blaise Pascal built a box full of gears to help him add numbers. In the twentieth century, scientists built powerful computers. At first they were very big, but gradually they got smaller. Today computers help us solve all kinds of problems. They also help us communicate faster than ever before on the Internet.

Activity 4. Optional: The World of Computers *(Online)*
Instructions
With your student, explore the fascinating world of computers at the highly interactive website, The Journey Inside.

The Journey Inside is made up of six lessons. For today, your student should complete parts 1, 2, 6, and 7 of the Intro to Computers lesson only. If your student is interested, the remaining parts and lessons can be completed later.

Activity 5. Optional: A Computer Revolution *(Online)*
Instructions
Have your student do some research online to learn about the origin of the term "computer bug."

Learning Coach Guide
Lesson 8: We Will Go to the Moon

The lunar landing on July 20, 1969 grew out of Cold War competition. The Soviets had launched the first unmanned satellite, Sputnik, and followed it with a manned space flight. John F. Kennedy committed the United States to land a man on the moon. When Neil Armstrong stepped on to the surface of the moon, that age-old dream was realized.

Lesson Objectives

- Explain that the space age began when the Soviet Union launched *Sputnik*, the first man-made satellite to orbit Earth.
- Identify John F. Kennedy as the president who committed the United States to landing a man on the moon.
- Identify the Apollo program as the U.S. space program that put a man on the moon, and recognize the Apollo 11 mission as the first to reach the moon.
- Name Neil Armstrong as the first person to walk on the moon.

PREPARE

Approximate lesson time is 60 minutes.

Keywords and Pronunciation

satellite : An object that orbits a planet.

Sputnik (SPUT-nik)

TEACH
Activity 1: A Man on the Moon *(Online)*
Instructions
This main teaching activity is online. Your student may complete this activity alone or with your help.

Activity 2: History Journal *(Offline)*
Instructions
With your student, read the History Journal entry for today's lesson and compare it with the sample paragraph below. Did it include the most important parts of the lesson?

The United States was in a race with the Soviet Union to land the first man on the moon. At first the Soviet Union was ahead. It launched *Sputnik*, the first man-made satellite. Then President Kennedy said that the United States would land on the moon. Americans worked very hard on the Apollo program. Apollo 11 was the mission that put the first astronauts on the moon. Neil Armstrong was the very first person to walk on the moon.

Activity 3: To the Moon and Back *(Online)*
Instructions
Your student will play the To the Moon and Back game to reinforce lesson objectives.

ASSESS
Lesson Assessment: We Will Go to the Moon (*Online*)
Students will complete an online assessment based on the lesson objectives. The assessment will be scored by the computer. The attached answer key is the most current and may not coincide with previously printed guides.

TEACH
Activity 4. Optional: We Will Go to the Moon *(Online)*
Instructions
Explore with your student websites related to the Apollo program and Apollo 11 in particular.

Apollo 30th Anniversary

The Apollo Program: Apollo 11

Kennedy Space Center: Apollo 11

NASA Human Space Flight: Apollo 11

JSC Digital Image Collection: Apollo 11

NASA: Apollo 11 Image Gallery

Learning Coach Guide
Lesson 9. Optional: A Polish Pope and Eastern Europe

Poland was one of the nations behind the Iron Curtain during the Cold War. Communists robbed the Polish people of many freedoms, including the freedom to worship God. In 1979 a Polish pope named John Paul II visited his homeland. It was a visit that challenged communist rule and helped change the world.

Lesson Objectives

- Locate Poland on a map.
- Describe John Paul II as a Polish pope.
- Explain that the pope's trip to Poland encouraged the Polish people to resist communist rule.

PREPARE

Approximate lesson time is 60 minutes.

Materials

For the Student

🖥 Cold War Europe, 1962

Keywords and Pronunciation

Karol Wojtyla (KAH-ruhl voy-TIL-ah)

Pole : Someone who lives in Poland.

pope : The leader of the Catholic Church.

strike : Stopping work as a way of protesting against something you think is wrong.

union : A group that protects the rights of workers.

TEACH
Activity 1. Optional: Optional Lesson Instructions (Online)

Activity 2. Optional: Poland Under Soviet Rule (Online)
Instructions
This main teaching activity is online. Your student may complete this activity alone or with your help.

Activity 3. Optional: A Letter (Offline)
Instructions
Have your student write a letter about Pope John Paul's visit to Poland in 1979.

Learning Coach Guide
Lesson 10: The End of the Cold War

The Berlin Wall stood for decades as the most famous symbol of communist rule. In a speech in West Berlin, U.S. President Ronald Reagan challenged the Soviets to tear it down. The Wall was finally knocked down in 1989, bringing an end to the long Cold War.

Lesson Objectives

- Identify Ronald Reagan as the U.S. president who challenged the communists to tear down the Berlin Wall.
- State that the Cold War ended in 1989 when the Berlin Wall fell.
- Explain that the Soviet Union's communist empire collapsed and democracy came to Eastern Europe.

PREPARE

Approximate lesson time is 60 minutes.

Materials

For the Student

    History Journal

    ⌨ After the Cold War

    map, world

Keywords and Pronunciation

Mikhail Gorbachev (mih-kah-EEL gawr-buh-CHAWF)

TEACH
Activity 1: The Cold War Begins to Thaw *(Online)*

Instructions

This main teaching activity is online. Your student may want to complete this activity by himself, or you may want to join him at the computer as he reads about the end of the Cold War.

Activity 2: History Journal *(Offline)*

Instructions

With your student, read the History Journal entry for today's lesson and compare it with the sample paragraph below. Did it include the most important parts of the lesson?

The Cold War came to an end when the Berlin Wall fell in 1989. Ronald Reagan had told the communists to tear down the wall. He gave a famous speech at the Berlin Wall. Reagan said, "Mr. Gorbachev, tear down this wall!" The people in Eastern Europe wanted to be free. They finally got their freedom. The Soviet Union and its communist empire fell apart. Democracy spread across Europe.

Activity 3: After the Cold War *(Online)*

Instructions

Help your student compare a modern map of the world with a Cold War-era map to see the change in political boundaries that occurred as a result of the end of the Cold War and the fall of communism in Eastern Europe.

Note: To view the online map in a larger mode, move the cursor over the map and then click Expand button.

Answers:

1. President Ronald Reagan
2. Poland
3. 1989
4. Russia
5. 15
6. Russia, Estonia, Latvia, Lithuania, Belarus, Ukraine, Moldavia, Georgia, Armenia, Azerbaijan, Kazakhstan, Kirghizstan, Uzbekistan, Turkmenistan, Tajikistan

---

ASSESS

Lesson Assessment: The End of the Cold War (*Online*)

Students will complete an online assessment based on the lesson objectives. The assessment will be scored by the computer. The attached answer key is the most current and may not coincide with previously printed guides.

Learning Coach Guide
Lesson 11: Unit Review and Assessment

The student will review this unit and take the unit assessment.

Lesson Objectives

- Demonstrate mastery of important knowledge and skills in this unit.
- Explain that Harry Truman thought the best chance for lasting peace was to help war-torn nations rebuild with sound economies and democratic governments.
- Describe the Marshall Plan as the U.S. plan to help rebuild Europe.
- Describe the United Nations as an international organization formed to promote world peace.
- Explain that the UN was founded at the end of World War II to encourage cooperation among nations.
- Name Eleanor Roosevelt as the person who led the effort to write the Universal Declaration of Human Rights.
- Identify Mohandas Gandhi as the leader of the movement for Indian independence.
- Explain that Gandhi used peaceful resistance to oppose British rule, and give one example of that technique (such as fasting, the Salt March, or wearing Indian cloth instead of British cloth).
- Explain that after World War II, European colonial empires began to disappear.
- Describe the Cold War as a dangerous period of rivalry between the United States and the Soviet Union.
- Explain that as chief rivals in the Cold War, the Soviet Union led communist nations and the United States led democratic nations.
- Explain that each side built nuclear weapons, which implied the threat of a third world war.
- Explain that the Berlin Wall was a wall erected by communists to keep people in East Berlin.
- Describe Mao Zedong as the leader who made China a Communist nation.
- Identify Jonas Salk as the creator of a vaccine to prevent polio.
- Identify John F. Kennedy as the president who committed the United States to landing a man on the moon.
- Name Neil Armstrong as the first person to walk on the moon.
- Identify Ronald Reagan as the U.S. president who challenged the communists to tear down the Berlin Wall.
- State that the Cold War ended in 1989 when the Berlin Wall fell.
- Explain that the Soviet Union's communist empire collapsed and democracy came to Eastern Europe.
- Explain that the post-war period was a time of advance in medicine and technology and name some of these advances (such as polio vaccine, lunar landing and space travel).

PREPARE

Approximate lesson time is 60 minutes.

TEACH

Activity 1: Rebuilding a Better World *(Offline)*

Instructions

The student will review this unit and take the unit assessment.

Activity 2: History Journal Review *(Offline)*

Instructions

The student will use the History Journal to review for the unit assessment. You can help by asking questions based on the work in the journal.

Activity 3: Online Interactive Review *(Online)*

Instructions

The student will continue reviewing the unit by completing an online, interactive review.

ASSESS

Unit Assessment: Rebuilding a Better World *(Offline)*

Students will complete an offline Unit Assessment. Print the assessment and have students complete it on their own. Use the answer key to score the assessment, and then enter the results online. The attached answer key is the most current and may not coincide with previously printed guides.

Rebuilding a Better World

Name _____ Date _____

Rebuilding a Better World

Match the name of each person on the left with the correct description on the right. Write the correct letter on the blank line.

1. **C** Eleanor Roosevelt   A. led the Soviet Union during much of the Cold War

   D Mohandas Gandhi   B. committed the United States to landing a man on the moon

   A Joseph Stalin   C. led the effort to write the U.N. Declaration of Human Rights

   E Mao Zedong   D. led the movement for Indian independence

   B John F. Kennedy   E. made China a communist nation

2. How did the Marshall Plan help war-torn nations?

   (a) It built up their armies and fought the Soviet Union.

   ● It rebuilt their economies and strengthened democracy.

   (c) It brought new dictators to power and spread communism.

   (d) It allowed new colonies in Asia, Africa, and South America.

3. What did the United Nations Declaration of Human Rights do?

   ● It spelled out the rights that people all over the world should have.

   (b) It spelled out terms for peace for all nations after World War II.

   (c) It spelled out human rights for people in the Industrial Revolution.

   (d) It spelled out human rights for all nations after World War I.

4. How did Mohandas Gandhi lead India to independence from Great Britain?

   (a) By using "blood and iron" against the British

   (b) By keeping British ships out of India's ports

   (c) By wearing British clothes to show friendship

   ● By resisting British rule without violence

5. Which of the following statements is true?

   (a) After World War II, Europeans founded more colonies in Africa.

   (b) After World War II, European colonial empires began to grow.

   ● After World War II, European colonial empires began to break up.

   (d) After World War II, Europe's colonies started the United Nations.

6. Which of the following best describes the Cold War?

   ● A dangerous time of rivalry between the United States and the Soviet Union

   (b) A time when the United States and the Soviet Union fought with computers

   (c) A period when the rivalry between the United States and the Soviet Union ended

   (d) A dangerous time of nuclear war between the United States and the Soviet Union

7. Which of the following caused the greatest fear and was a threat to peace during the Cold War?

   (a) Large outbreaks of polio

   (b) The race to put men into space

   (c) The invention of new computers

   ● The build-up of nuclear weapons

8. During the Cold War, the Soviet Union led _____ nations, while the United States led _____ nations.

   (a) democratic; communist

   ● communist; democratic

   (c) colonial; communist

   (d) democratic; colonial

9. During the Cold War, China became a _____ country.

   (a) democratic

   ● communist

   (c) colonial

   (d) Catholic

10. Why did the communists build the Berlin Wall?

   (a) To keep the Soviet Union from sending more troops into East Berlin

   (b) To keep people in democratic West Berlin from escaping to East Berlin

   ● To keep people in communist East Berlin from escaping to West Berlin

   (d) To keep the United States from taking territory inside East Berlin

11. Which astronaut became the first person to set foot on the moon?

   (a) Edwin "Buzz" Aldrin

   ● Neil Armstrong

   (c) Jonas Salk

   (d) George Marshall

Rebuilding a Better World

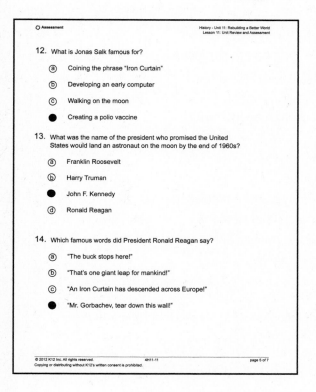

12. What is Jonas Salk famous for?

 ⓐ Coining the phrase "Iron Curtain"

 ⓑ Developing an early computer

 ⓒ Walking on the moon

 ● Creating a polio vaccine

13. What was the name of the president who promised the United States would land an astronaut on the moon by the end of 1960s?

 ⓐ Franklin Roosevelt

 ⓑ Harry Truman

 ● John F. Kennedy

 ⓓ Ronald Reagan

14. Which famous words did President Ronald Reagan say?

 ⓐ "The buck stops here!"

 ⓑ "That's one giant leap for mankind!"

 ⓒ "An Iron Curtain has descended across Europe!"

 ● "Mr. Gorbachev, tear down this wall!"

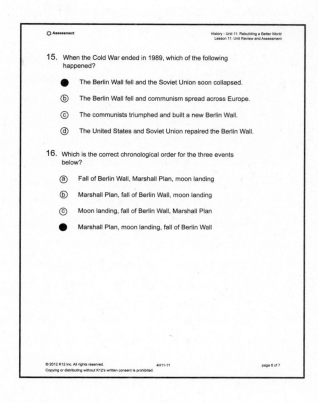

15. When the Cold War ended in 1989, which of the following happened?

 ● The Berlin Wall fell and the Soviet Union soon collapsed.

 ⓑ The Berlin Wall fell and communism spread across Europe.

 ⓒ The communists triumphed and built a new Berlin Wall.

 ⓓ The United States and Soviet Union repaired the Berlin Wall.

16. Which is the correct chronological order for the three events below?

 ⓐ Fall of Berlin Wall, Marshall Plan, moon landing

 ⓑ Marshall Plan, fall of Berlin Wall, moon landing

 ⓒ Moon landing, fall of Berlin Wall, Marshall Plan

 ● Marshall Plan, moon landing, fall of Berlin Wall

17. Essay Question

Write a paragraph telling how people tried to rebuild a better world after World War II. Begin with the sentence: "After World War II many people worked hard to make the world a better place."

Include the following:
• Tell why the United Nations was founded.
• Give one example of an advance in science or technology and explain why it was important.
• Give an example that shows that many people gained more freedom during these years.

_____
_____
_____
_____
_____
_____
_____
_____
_____
_____
_____
_____
_____
_____
_____
_____
_____

Scoring the Essay Question

This essay question is worth fifty points. Score the student's writing as follows:

• Ten points for stating the United Nations was founded to encourage peace (or cooperation among nations).

• Twenty points for naming the polio vaccine, the lunar landing, space travel, television, or computers as an example of advances in science or technology.

• Twenty points for stating any one of the following examples of people gaining freedom: India's independence from Great Britain; the disappearance of colonial empires; the collapse of the Soviet Union; the fall of the Berlin Wall; the collapse of communism; the spread of democracy in Eastern Europe.

Learning Coach Guide
Lesson 12: Final Review and Assessment

The student will take the semester assessment.

Lesson Objectives

- Demonstrate mastery of important knowledge and skills learned this semester.
- Demonstrate mastery of important knowledge and skills in this unit.
- Define *imperialism* as the drive to create empires overseas.
- Recognize Rudyard Kipling as a great British writer who wrote about India.
- Explain that Kipling wrote children's stories.
- Explain that Kipling celebrated the British Empire in his writings.
- Describe Edison as one of the greatest inventors of all time.
- Explain that Ford's assembly line factory made production faster and cheaper.
- State that the first successful flight occurred at Kitty Hawk, North Carolina.
- Describe the Panama Canal as a waterway connecting the Atlantic and Pacific Oceans.
- State that the "the Great War" was the term used to describe World War I.
- Recognize that "make the world safe for democracy" was a United States slogan in World War I and a reason for entering the war.
- Explain that Woodrow Wilson proposed the League of Nations to stop future wars, and that the United States did not join the League.
- Describe the woman's suffrage movement as the movement for the right of women to vote.
- Describe Charles Lindbergh as the first man to fly solo across the Atlantic Ocean.
- Identify Alexander Fleming as the British scientist who discovered penicillin.
- Identify Franklin Delano Roosevelt as president of the United States during the Great Depression.
- Explain that World War I left many problems unsolved and the Great Depression affected the whole world.
- Identify Stalin, Hitler, and Mussolini as dictators who led the Soviet Union, Germany, and Italy.
- Explain that Churchill led Great Britain through the Battle of Britain.
- Describe the Holocaust as the mass murder of millions of Jews by the Nazis.
- Explain that the Japanese launched a surprise attack on the U.S. Naval Base at Pearl Harbor in Hawaii on December 7, 1941.
- Explain that the United States used the atomic bomb on Hiroshima and Nagasaki to end the war.
- Explain that Harry Truman thought the best chance for lasting peace was to help war-torn nations rebuild with sound economies and democratic governments.
- Describe the United Nations as an international organization formed to promote world peace.
- Name Eleanor Roosevelt as the person who led the effort to write the Universal Declaration of Human Rights.
- Explain that Gandhi used peaceful resistance to oppose British rule, and give one example of that technique (such as fasting, the Salt March, or wearing Indian cloth instead of British cloth).
- Identify Jonas Salk as the creator of a vaccine to prevent polio.

- Identify John F. Kennedy as the president who committed the United States to landing a man on the moon.
- Identify Ronald Reagan as the U.S. president who challenged the communists to tear down the Berlin Wall.
- Describe the late nineteenth and early twentieth centuries as an age of invention and enterprise.
- Describe the Russian Revolution as one that involved the overthrow of the czar and the triumph of Communism.

PREPARE

Approximate lesson time is 60 minutes.

TEACH

Activity 1: Rebuilding a Better World (Offline)

Activity 2: End of Semester (Online)

ASSESS

Semester Assessment: History 4, Semester 2 (Offline)

Students will complete an offline Semester assessment. Print the assessment and have students complete it on their own. Use the answer key to score the assessment, and then enter the results online. The attached answer key is the most current and may not coincide with previously printed guides.

Final Review and Assessment

Name _____ Date _____

Final Review and Assessment

Match the item on the left with the reason it is important on the right. Write the correct letter on the blank line.

1. **D** Pearl Harbor

   A. imaginary barrier between communist and democratic lands

   C Kitty Hawk, North Carolina

   B. site of famous World War I battles

   B Flanders Fields

   C. location of the first successful airplane flight

   E Hiroshima

   D. U.S. naval base attacked by the Japanese

   A Iron Curtain

   E. city where the first atomic bomb was dropped

Read each question and its answer choices. Fill in the bubble in front of the best answer.

2. What does the "Age of Imperialism" refer to?

   ⓐ A time when democratic nations became industrial

   ⓑ A period when Gandhi and Mao fought for larger Asian empires

   ● A time when industrial nations established colonies overseas

   ⓓ A period of invention and innovation in medicine and industry

3. This British writer lived in India, wrote children's stories, and was proud of the British empire. Who was he?

   ● Rudyard Kipling

   ⓑ Winston Churchill

   ⓒ David Livingstone

   ⓓ Alexander Graham Bell

4. The lightbulb and phonograph have been invented. Mr. Bell has placed a telephone call. Mr. Andrew Carnegie is now making a fortune in steel. What year is it?

   ⓐ 1800

   ● 1900

   ⓒ 1950

   ⓓ 1776

5. The assembly line I developed made it much easier and much cheaper to produce cars. Who am I?

   ● Henry Ford

   ⓑ Karl Daimler

   ⓒ Andrew Carnegie

   ⓓ Louis Pasteur

6. Which of the following describes Thomas Edison?

   ⓐ Chief engineer of the Panama Canal

   ● Ingenious inventor, known as "the Wizard of Menlo Park"

   ⓒ Designer of the first airplane, regarded as "the first in flight"

   ⓓ Chemist who figured out how to kill harmful bacteria

7. Which bodies of water does the Panama Canal connect?

   ⓐ Mediterranean and Red Seas

   ⓑ Yellow and Yangtze Rivers

   ⓒ Atlantic Ocean and Great Lakes

   ● Atlantic and Pacific Oceans

8. Which war was called "the Great War" or "the war to make the world safe for democracy"?

   ⓐ World War II

   ● World War I

   ⓒ The Spanish-American War

   ⓓ The Cold War

9. What does women's suffrage refer to?

   ● The right of women to vote

   ⓑ The ability of women to suffer silently

   ⓒ The vaccination of women against polio

   ⓓ The right of women to protest

10. How can we describe the peace that followed World War I?

    ⓐ A time of prosperity and international cooperation

    ● A time of resentment, depression, and unrest

    ⓒ A time of new democratic gains in Germany and Italy

    ⓓ A time of nuclear threat and east-west tension

11. Who were Hitler, Mussolini, and Stalin?

    ⓐ Communists who began the Cold War

    ⓑ Founders of the United Nations

    ● Dictators who came to power in the 1930s

    ⓓ Leaders in the war against tyranny

Final Review and Assessment

12. What do Alexander Fleming and Jonas Salk have in common?

- ● They were both pioneers in medicine.
- ⓑ They were both leaders of independence movements.
- ⓒ They were both inventors who modernized cities.
- ⓓ They were both helpful with the Marshall Plan.

13. What were the League of Nations and the United Nations?

- ⓐ Alliances formed in time of war
- ● International organizations formed to promote peace
- ⓒ Anti-colonial movements against European powers
- ⓓ Medical organizations providing disaster relief

14. In her later life, Eleanor Roosevelt worked with the United Nations to

- ⓐ advocate space travel.
- ● promote human rights.
- ⓒ get computers in schools.
- ⓓ end British rule in India.

4H11-12

15. Even though there was a lot of war and bloodshed in the twentieth century, there was also

- ● great progress in communication, transportation, and medicine.
- ⓑ peace and good will for most people of eastern Europe.
- ⓒ growing awareness that communism brought prosperity to its citizens.
- ⓓ an important treaty that eliminated all nuclear weapons.

16. He led the United States through the Great Depression and most of World War II. Who was he?

- ⓐ Harry Truman
- ⓑ John F. Kennedy
- ⓒ Ronald Reagan
- ● Franklin Roosevelt

17. In 1957 the Soviet Union sent *Sputnik*, the first man-made satellite, into space. President John F. Kennedy responded by urging the United States to

- ⓐ send a missile to shoot down the Soviet satellite
- ● land a man on the moon before the end of the 1960s
- ⓒ cooperate with the Soviet Union in developing new spacecraft
- ⓓ send troops to attack the Soviet Union

4H11-12

18. One of the greatest horrors of World War II was Hitler's attempt to kill all the Jews in Europe. What was that attempt called?

- ⓐ D-Day
- ⓑ *Blitzkrieg*
- ⓒ The Cold War
- ● The Holocaust

19. What was Mohandas Gandhi's Salt March?

- ● Part of a campaign to free India from British Rule
- ⓑ A military march from Calcutta to Delhi
- ⓒ Part of a campaign to institute communism in India
- ⓓ An attempt to supply India with salt from the ocean

20. Which American president said, "Mr. Gorbachev, tear down this wall"?

- ⓐ Franklin Roosevelt
- ⓑ Harry Truman
- ⓒ John F. Kennedy
- ● Ronald Reagan

4H11-12

21. At the end of World War II, what did the victors do?

- ⓐ They forced Germany, Italy, and Japan to pay reparations for their evil deeds.
- ⓑ They turned Africa and Asia into colonial empires under Allied rule.
- ⓒ They divided up the land of the Axis powers and kept it for themselves.
- ● They helped rebuild the economies and governments of war-torn nations.

22. What do we call the time when Czar Nicholas was ousted and Lenin came to power?

- ● The Russian Revolution
- ⓑ The Cultural Revolution
- ⓒ The Cold War
- ⓓ The Soviet Supremacy

23. Who led the British during the Battle of Britain and proved to be one of the greatest leaders England ever had?

- ⓐ David Livingstone
- ● Winston Churchhill
- ⓒ Queen Victoria
- ⓓ Dwight Eisenhower

4H11-12

Final Review and Assessment

24. How did Charles Lindbergh lift people's spirits in the 1920s?

   (a) He invented the first antibiotic.

   ● He flew solo between New York and Paris.

   (c) He became a champion flagpole sitter.

   (d) He discovered a way to make computers small.

25. What have the governments of Lenin, Stalin, and Mao shown about communism?

   (a) It tends to make people free and increase their standard of living.

   (b) It encourages religious worship and promotes great art.

   ● It puts power in the hands of few, and takes freedom away from many.

   (d) It does not encourage advances in science or technology.

26. The Cold War ended when the Berlin Wall fell and the Soviet Union broke apart. Why were people so happy the Cold War ended?

   (a) There was less threat of another world war.

   (b) There was a greater chance for freedom and democracy in Eastern Europe and elsewhere.

   (c) The deadly threat of communism was over.

   ● All of the above

4H11-12